POWER OF 4

POWER OF 4

How Christian Men
Create Purposeful Lives
By Not Going it Alone

MARK WARREN *and*
DR. STEVEN D. BAGLEY
with Michael Ashley

www.powerof4.co

Published by www.powerof4.co

ISBN: 979-8-36448-999-9

Interior book design by Claudine Mansour Design

First Edition

Printed in the United States of America

*To the fellas and brothers who have
come ugly over the years.
We salute your commitment to the Lord,
and we are praying for you.*

CONTENTS

Author's Note

Wherever and whenever needed, we modified non-essential facts/details to protect current and past Power of 4 brothers and/or their families.

FOREWORD

"No man is an island," observed the famous Cambridge divine, John Donne. Donne, a preacher at St. Paul's Cathedral in London, used the metaphor of a continent to show that even islands are situated as part of the larger whole:

No man is an island,
Entire of itself;
Every man is a piece of the continent,
A part of the main.

But Donne didn't just have in mind eschewing loneliness or isolation in favor of promoting the universality of mankind. Inspired by God's fashioning humanity in the context of strong communities, beginning with the family, Donne was saying that a man is more substantial when intentionally bonded to another, especially with other men of purpose. "Though a man might prevail against one who is alone, two will withstand him—a threefold cord is not quickly broken (Ecclesiastes 4:12, ESV)." If two is good, writes the Teacher, then three is better. And not just better, but stronger. The authors of this book embrace these biblical maxims and advance a further divine building block: "Power of 4."

The power of 4, of course, has been woven into the order of creation itself, connoting structure, balance, logic, and strength. God established four seasons, the four phases of the moon, the four points of the compass, and four basic elements of earth, air, fire, and water.

What's more, the Word of God exhibits "Power of 4" in relational contexts among men, setting forth no greater example than Jesus and his "inner circle" of Peter, James, and John. Men trooped in four have the perspective to see in all directions (minimizing blind spots), multiply gifts and experiences, and augment the strength of their brothers fourfold.

The past two decades have seen lots of ink spilled on the need to recover a distinctly virtuous masculinity, embodying principles by which men of earlier generations would, by the hundreds of thousands, give their bodies and lives to noble endeavors in defense of freedom and the promotion of what was good, true, and beautiful. While astutely descriptive of the "masculinity crisis" exacerbated by cultural disruptors ranging from "free love" and "feminism" to "the war on men" and "a cult of narcissism," few of these books contributed real-world solutions. In this way, *Power of 4* is uniquely prescriptive, though not in such a way that it leaves a man alone with his thoughts, but resorting to Power of 4.

The idea of "Power of 4" is predicated upon the fact that ours is a narratable existence, that we live in a narratable world. Each of us has a story and we live storied lives. Power of 4 isn't so much a narrative but a domain of masculine narration, where the values, institutions, vocations, and symbols of masculinity have free course among four men before the face of the living God. This is to say that Power of 4 is itself subsumed within the grand narrative of God's creative presence, activity, authority, and purposes in the storied lives of men.

It begins with a recognition of God's self-disclosure in distinctly masculine categories. The Creator God is known as "Father." The Father is such because of the ever-begotten Son. He who sees the Son, sees the Father (John 14:9). And it is the Son, in the wisdom and power of the Holy Spirit, who appoints men to be *his* representatives: "The one who hears you hears me, and the one who rejects you rejects me, and the one who rejects me rejects him who sent me (Luke 10:16, ESV)."

The authors of *Power of 4* are not content to merely stimulate Christian thought but rather to inspire Christian action toward change in American culture, beginning with men's roles. They do so with a spirit of energizing optimism amidst what they describe as the cultural battle for Western civilization.

So far from hand-wringing over the seismic shift away from America's original Judeo-Christian values that grounded principles of freedom, justice, and human dignity in a transcendent and divine framework, these men believe something can be done about halting and correcting America's trajectory of ideological and moral decay. This decay, they observe, has eviscerated biblical masculinity in the likeness of Christ Jesus to such a degree as to be a cowardly and confused shell of itself. *Power of 4* is their call to action.

So, while philosopher Charles Taylor argues in *A Secular Age* that godless secularism and shallow consumerism is here to stay, the authors say that may be so, but it doesn't mean any more ground need be surrendered to secularism and consumerism and the dehumanizing, liberty-effacing values that come with them.

The authors of this book recognize that the biblical doctrine of *vocation*, highlighted in the sixteenth century by Martin Luther, is essential to masculinity. In fact, vocation defines masculinity. Just as the Father is represented by the Son, that is, it is the Son's vocation to be the image/icon of the Father (Colossians 1:15), so too it is the vocation of men to image forth or be iconic of the Son's masculine vocations in relation to his Father in heaven, his brothers on earth, his bride (the Church), as neighbor to fellow citizens, and as the King (not queen) over the Kingdom of God.

Jesus does this in the power of the Holy Spirit.

Power of 4 aids men in *being* masculine in accordance with their God-given vocations, not with *acting* masculine. What's more, a commonsense and theologically correct understanding of masculinity stipulates that no one knows a man, with all of his weaknesses, failings, problems, and challenges, but also potential and powers quite like another man. A recovered and strengthened masculinity owns its God-given biological sex and corresponding maleness, and resorts to it for its strengthening and advancement, but also correction and healing, taking its cues from the archetypal man, Jesus of Nazareth. A man's various vocations emerge from their inherent and constitutive masculinity beginning with the creation of man and confirmed in the incarnation of the Son of the Father. Within the context of Power of 4, these men believe, teach, and confess these vocational realities as foundational to principled masculinity.

True masculinity, in contradistinction to toxic, selfish masculinity, is about love for those for whom it is our privilege to love. Love, then, forms truly masculine habits. And the habit to be cultivated above all is to be present as sons, brothers, husbands, and fathers. These are God-given vocations, and they trump any other supposed obligation.

The authors' principal summons to bond together in manly friendship entails personal sacrifice for the edification of the other. In an age of self-aggrandizing, narcissism, and victimization, such a call requires risk, courage, and honesty—all deeply masculine traits. Power of 4 welcomes men with all their self-imposed or otherwise embraced "ugliness" to repent, confess, and receive absolution. It turns out Power of 4 is bound up with the power of forgiveness, which in turn unburdens men and empowers them.

This may not seem like such a big deal. After all, it's just a few words of apology and pardon, but the authors know that words "do things." The performative speech act of forgiveness creates a new state of affairs, a new reality obtains, and now, by God's grace, we can boldly live before God. We can confidently live with our wives and children; we can even live with ourselves. Forgiveness restores and it restores man to his God-given vocations, empowering him to change and for change. Power of 4 facilitates this from a man to a man in the presence of manly witnesses, in the name of the living God.

Such sacrifice means men no longer taking the easy route of capitulation or passivity or, indeed, apathy, but instead asserting oneself into those domains of influence that can effect change—marriage, family, friendships, and work. That may and likely will come with some sacrificial cost. Positively, Christians have civic obligations concomitant to their various God-given vocations, which includes virtuous citizenry. Christians, stated plainly, have a duty to be patriots and exemplary citizens who influence society for the good and toward the good.

The authors set forth a model for change reminiscent of eighteenth-century British parliamentarian and philosopher Edmund Burke, who advocated for "little platoons." "Little platoons" begin, foremost, with strong men in good marriages and loving families, then increase in spheres of influence and numbers with vibrant churches, fraternal groups, and various neighborhood and community associations, through which all Christians, indeed, all citizens, can participate in various specific acts to make possible the renewal of Western society. The building block of any little platoon

(Marine Corps fire units are members of 4, so that they may have perspective in all directions) or the most irreducible domain for the recovery of masculinity is Power of 4.

Power of 4 only has viability if it maintains fidelity to a cause: the promotion and defense of that which is good, true, and beautiful. It has a telos, namely promoting a spirit of masculinity driven by a cause known and believed—specifically that God created men to fill male vocations that image forth his fatherliness. This makes these men, trooped before God, fundamentally different than an Accountability Group or Mastermind Group or Bible Study Group. As a bond of sacred trust, facilitating the multifaceted perspective of men deeply invested in the welfare of their brothers, they begin with a man's attitude toward duty, that is, toward his God-given vocations as a man, son, brother, husband, father, and citizen—and they stay focused on that. Power of 4 develops with a man's command over himself or his failure to do so. Either way, there can be little argument that the original four of Christ and his "inner circle" were altered by their God-given vocations and, in turn, careened the story of the world into a fresh and much-needed direction.

— Reverend John J Bombaro, PhD, CDR, CHC;
US Navy Reserve and Assistant Director of Theological
Education at the Luther Academy, Rīga, Latvia

POWER OF 4

PART

1

THE PROBLEM

We establish the universal dilemma
so many men face, introducing the
need for a Power of 4.

CHAPTER 1

I've Had This Problem About Being a Man Since I Was a Kid

Millions upon millions of men struggle with the same crisis. *Masculinity*. The catastrophe respects no boundaries. It crosses generations, financial and class status, race, and every other way we segment ourselves. One of the insidious aspects of this crisis—and make no mistake, it *is* a crisis—is that it's quite uncommon for two men to express their frustrations about it the same way.

Some men feel like no matter how much wind they have in their sails, they cannot steer a course due to a bad rudder. Others, the car guys, know their engine is running fine, but they've stripped gears out of their transmission, so all that power never translates to rubber meeting the road. No matter how a man expresses his dilemma, what he says can be boiled down to a core problem, one this book will help you address—hopefully with the help of three other men working as a team.

For, no matter how a man describes feeling lost and directionless, what he's really saying is that he senses a lack of genuine interaction with others. Instead of being real people—*real men*—we males find ourselves playing roles we believe we're supposed to fill, whether they fit us or not. If and when a man realizes, even on a subconscious level, that his actual character, his authentic masculinity, has been replaced by a hollow shadow play, he's bound to feel uncomfortable. Lost. Adrift. Depressed. Abandoned.

We don't blame him. Instead, we can help him. Beginning with this book. But what follows isn't some dry academic treatise. So, let's get right to an example of how one man expressed such dissatisfaction with playing a role. It's critical because it led to the forming of our men's group: Power of 4.

THE HADDIE STORY

Let's set the scene. Power of 4 cofounder and coauthor Steve Bagley once attended a Christmas party hosted by fellow cofounder and coauthor Mark Warren. Mark mesmerized the group with a tale that would impact both men's lives more than they could have ever predicted.

It went like this:

> As you all know, we're the typical suburban family. There's me, who's always working, my lovely wife Margy, and our two kids, Jessie and Luke. As many of you know, I'm at the office before the sun is up and rarely home before it's down. Okay, okay. Yes, I'm a workaholic, but it takes sacrifices to be a good provider.
>
> Anyway, most days Margy gets the kids ready for school after taking our dog Haddie on a walk around the block. That *was* their routine. Until last week— the day Haddie got loose.
>
> Late for work, our neighbor backed his car out of the garage without looking back, crushing poor Haddie to death. Margy happened to open the front door

at just that precise moment and saw it all happen. It was beyond awful!

Margy was in shock, and with "perfect" timing, the kids ran out to catch the bus just seconds after Haddie took her last breath. Poor Margy. It was all she could do to keep the kids from seeing our dog's lifeless body. Without thinking, she blurted out to them, "Haddie's dead!"

But she wasn't ready for what happened next. The kids merely waved and smiled. "Okay, Mom," they said. "See you after school!"

Margy couldn't believe it. *The kids misheard her anguished cry about Haddie.* They must have thought she said, "Have a good day," like she always did as they boarded the bus.

Margy thought this was good. The kids wouldn't have their day at school ruined. She had time to plan a burial for Haddie *and* mentally prepare to tell them the bad news. For real, this time.

As usual, the kids' bus dropped them off at 3:00 p.m. and Margy was ready. She had spent hours rehearsing a little speech to help her little ones understand and grapple with the tragedy.

But by the time the bus pulled up, she opted to just give it to them straight. "Kids," she began, "this morning Haddie was hit by a car. Don't worry. She died instantly and I'm sure she's gone to heaven."

The shock and horror on their faces broke Margy's heart. She must have been correct that morning when she guessed they hadn't heard her.

Jessie and Luke both cried out at the same time: "*Haddie?* We thought you said 'Daddy!'"

The whole room broke out in laughter, a mix of Mark's natural storytelling abilities and a punchline that could have come from any TV show with some bumbling dad, like *Married . . . With Children.* Steve chuckled along with the others, but a part of him remained serious. Unlike the others, he suspected Mark was making a deeper point. This was confirmed when one partygoer who had a few too many that night, asked if all that was true.

"Nah," Mark replied. "It's just a signature story to make a point."

Mark's point? He saw himself in that joke. In his own words, "The Haddie story was the crux of a life where my drugs of choice were accomplishment and accumulation." This resonated with Steve, who saw himself similarly. Mark and Steve were each playing *roles* as men. And not feeling so great about it.

In his 30s at the time, Mark lived in San Juan Capistrano, California, with Margy, his homemaker wife, and two small kids. (Though they didn't have a dog named Haddie.) Like he admitted, Mark worked insane hours. Launching an investment management business throughout the West Coast, he traveled three days a week, amounting to 120 nights a year away from home.

Although Mark told the Haddie joke to much laughter, Steve couldn't help feeling there was an uncomfortable amount of truth to it. Truth about his own life. You see, while Mark was busy flying around the country, Steve was pouring his time into a counseling service he launched with his wife. He put an astounding number of miles on his Lexus. But this vehicle wasn't just for transportation. It was also his office. His lunch table. Even his bed sometimes, though he claims he never spent the night in it.

Essentially, both men were road warriors desperately trying

to achieve material success. And both saw thems
Haddie joke. Mark would be the first to admit t
was playing the role of "provider" as best he cou
knew in his heart he wasn't being true to himself.

Mark wasn't alone in this insecurity. It was and is felt by
millions of men throughout the country. And, although
many cultural factors contribute to the crisis, the root cause
can be found in a surprising place: World War II.

HOW WORLD WAR II
SCREWED UP MASCULINITY

The casualties of World War II boggle the mind. According
to World-War-2.info, an internet clearinghouse for reliable
data, more than 16 million Americans served in the armed
forces during the conflict, with 405,399 killed in action and
671,278 wounded. It's nearly impossible to comprehend
these numbers because they are just so huge. Another way
to understand American sacrifices is to note that every small
town in America has a war memorial listing those citizens
that gave their lives for our freedom. In World War II, those
young men often died in European towns whose names they
would have trouble pronouncing, or on Pacific islands that
they had never heard of.

For those who did survive and return in one piece, they
found our culture had moved on without them. Troops were
expected to transition from the horrors of the Battle of the
Bulge and the beaches of Saipan to become soldiers of a
different type. They were to engage in *economic warfare* with
sights set on a booming post-war economy.

And yet, at the same time, women in the mold of "Rosie the
Riveter" were also suddenly expected to drop their wartime
roles to return to being "good housewives." By no means was

this a smooth transition, as described by Jorden Pitt for the National WWII Museum:

> Moreover, at war's end, changing social emphasis from war to peace prompted new ideas of manhood better suited for peacetime. Indeed, the war catalyzed a change that shifted the focus from the "tough" characteristics of masculinity to the need for veterans to create an idyllic postwar life with a family and a stable job. In short, the time had now come for these men to become good American citizens and contribute to the nation's postwar advancement. However, the war's physical and psychological legacies often made it difficult for men to reintegrate into civilian life and fulfill these duties.

The war challenged prevailing ideas of manhood in part because war required women's participation, both civilian and military. As military service pulled men from industrial work, women began performing those roles to contribute to the war effort.

As historian Elaine Tyler May writes, "The war emergency required the society to restructure itself and opened the way for the emancipation of women on an unprecedented scale." American society promoted women's expanded roles as a form of patriotism, but as soon as the war ended, many Americans expected women to return to the home to fulfill their domestic duties to prepare themselves for the time when they became wives and mothers. Employers now pushed women from higher-paying and secure wartime jobs to the service sector to make way for returning veterans. Thus, entering the workforce and becoming fathers and husbands now became the hallmarks of American masculinity after the war.

Although official statistics list more than 671,000 Americans wounded in World War II, this number would be much higher if it included veterans with emotional and psychological scars following their service. Many men came back incapable of playing their role in the American post-war economic miracle. This was often due to psychological and emotional problems that were not as well understood then as they are today. According to the Department of Veterans Affairs (V.A.), post-traumatic stress disorder (PTSD) was not recognized by the American Psychiatric Association until 1980, meaning that when vets experienced psychological problems due to the horrors of war, it was frequently blamed on "inherent individual weakness."

Psychiatrists who worked with thousands of veterans noted that emotional problems created "inferiority feelings or socially unadapted behavior." Here's an example of the latter. Some men who felt they couldn't adjust to the social norms of post-war America founded the "motorcycle clubs" that devolved into notorious biker gangs. As noted by Tony Tekaroniake Evans writing for History.com, scholar William Dulaney wrote: "It seems logical that the horrors of war and the hell of combat may have melted down the prewar personalities of these men, only to recast them forever in a new form."

In many cases, men found themselves pushed out of *self-healing*, once a key aspect of masculinity. What's more, pop culture relentlessly emphasized the concept of women as healers of men. Scholar Christina Jarvis describes this phenomenon when she writes: "[This] focus on women's agency ... often leads to an erasure of men's own self-healing powers and to readings that obscure the consolidation of male power in postwar America."

Due in part to this cultural shift, men could no longer demonstrate their masculinity by healing themselves, or even "recasting themselves," to use Dulaney's wording. Instead, they relied on women to restore their masculinity as a kind of "Florence Nightingale," but for the spirit.

GENDER ROLE BREAKDOWN

This emphasis on women healing men wasn't the only big change concerning females, both during and after the war. During hostilities women faced the very real prospect of their men leaving and never returning. Yet unlike soldiers in Europe or the Pacific islands, American men were not defending a homeland. They were traveling around the world to fight and possibly die for their country.

As the men left, women were expected to fill gaps. Most of us know about "Rosie the Riveter," a symbol for women tasked with factory work to power the Allied war machine. What many don't realize is that women didn't just fill the factories. They performed in many other lines of work, transforming our nation's economic course.

To their credit, women in America sprung to action as if their men would never return. Along with traditional male tasks, like working outside the home, they took over raising the next generation of males. This wasn't only the case in families where the father fell in battle, either. It was far more widespread due to the influx of women teaching boys in school. School headmasters, once a male role model for boys, vanished as men were called up for service. The net result? This left the next generation to be educated almost *exclusively* by women.

Educational activist group The Edvocate explains that during the war, "More women were offered opportunities for education, and many found employment in the teaching field." The Lanham Act of 1941 enabled this shift by making federal aid available to districts overrun with students at the same time male teachers left for military service. Naturally, most, if not all, those teachers hired with this governmental largesse were women.

Men did make a comeback in education after the war as the G.I. Bill afforded veterans the chance to earn a college degree. Even so, vast female representation was now firmly in place. This trend has only continued over the last few decades as the percentage of male teachers has markedly declined.

FALLOUT

For the post-war generation of baby boomers, like Mark, women raising men led to unforeseen problems. What's the result of such education without an appropriate male role model? Profound confusion and insecurity metastasizing throughout various phases of a man's life, for one thing. Men like Mark did not leave childhood with a sense of confidence based on a clear male/female family dynamic. Rather, they experienced profound anxiety about what masculinity meant. This led many young men to inhabit roles they perceived to be the *correct* manifestation of masculinity. Even if these were harmful and far from correct. In short, it led post-war men off purpose.

This societal shift has demoralized men in the 70 years since World War II. Consider the words of *Fight Club*'s main character, Tyler Durden. Played by Brad Pitt in the 1999 film, Durden captures male generational malaise with this evocative language: "We're a generation of men raised by women.

I'm wondering if another woman is really the answer we need."

It should be noted that the author of the novel *Fight Club*, Chuck Palahniuk, was born on the cusp of the "Boomer Generation" and "Generation X" (Gen X). His Durden character is describing what happened to so many men raised in a vacuum of male influence. It's sadly telling that the way they handle life's problems is to meet in secret underground facilities to beat up other men—and get beat up themselves.

Palahniuk further exposed the trouble with modern masculinity in an interview discussing *Fight Club's* popularity. "[There are] all these different models in which women can come together and talk about their lives. And if you're a man, you've got either fight club, or you have the Dead Poets Society. So, we don't have a lot of narratives . . . or a kind of script in which men come together and talk about their [lives]."

They don't have Power of 4.

But first, to be clear, the damage female-administered education has wrought upon masculinity is cross-generational. And its severity can't be overstated. This is also because schools were *already* harming boys long before women took over the halls of learning. Schoolteacher John Taylor Gatto, author of *Dumbing Us Down*, once wrote: "I feel ashamed that so many of us cannot imagine a better way to do things than locking children up all day in cells instead of letting them grow up knowing their families, mingling with the world, assuming real obligations, striving to be independent and self-reliant and free."

Gatto isn't alone in his assessment. As historian Geoffrey Botkin documented for the Western Conservatory of the Arts and Sciences, one influencer thinker of the 1860s, Herbert Spencer, said school, "Deprived children of raw experience and responsibility precisely at the moment their natural development demanded it, and that this experience and responsibility could not be made up for later."

If you're reading this book, you probably already suspect our masculinity crisis goes far beyond schools, workforce transformations, and a paucity of male role models. Many factors contribute to the mess we are in, but several big ones stand out the most. Just as the book of Revelation describes the Four Horsemen of the Apocalypse, America experienced four cultural disruptors that left masculinity on the ropes. Before we go into them, let's describe the problem a bit more.

DISRUPTED CULTURE, DISRUPTED LIVES

As mentioned, during World War II, women took over traditional male roles in their absence. Naturally, some females soon began to wonder, "Why do I need a man at all?" Whether or not you think this is a fair question, it was on the minds of millions of women, whether they were getting splattered with grease in a munitions factory, teaching a class full of raucous boys, or working the farm. This mentality led to a schism between the sexes that has only widened—and worsened—each decade. One sign of this rift is the difference in how men and women approach careers in fields traditionally dominated by one sex.

As documented by business publication *Fast Company*, women have made rapid advances in once male-oriented fields, especially in recent years. These include high-paying careers like the practice of law, medicine, and high finance. On the other hand, men haven't enjoyed such an equal uptick in female-dominated fields like teaching, nursing, and human resources.

There are several explanations for this phenomenon. For one, some men feel participating in female-dominated careers degrades their masculinity. We tend to discount this factor, as there is a precedent of men in education, stretching back to this country's founding. The second argument for men not entering female-dominated careers is that they tend to pay less. It's understandable that a man would pursue a lucrative career in Silicon Valley over education, but teaching is not necessarily a poorly compensated career. Not only do teachers' unions negotiate higher salaries, but teachers also have summers off to engage in other lines of work, or even to take an extended vacation.

But where this argument really breaks down is in the case of nursing.

As we know, nurses save lives. There is nothing intrinsically feminine about that. Also, nurses are typically well compensated. And yet, there now exists such a lack of nurses in America that hospitals will practically throw money at qualified staff to pick up shifts. Even so, *Fast Company* reveals only 13% of nurses are men. This astonishing fact doesn't necessarily concern market forces or men being reluctant to do "feminine work."

It points to a very serious schism between the sexes. We don't have to look as far back as the 1960s to see dramatic changes in our culture and our families. Seismic domestic transformations have occurred, particularly since the 1990s. If you haven't seen this with your own eyes, consider data on who heads up households and who brings home the bacon nowadays.

The traditional concept of a married man acting as head of household and breadwinner are on life support, if not already dead and buried. According to the Urban Institute, between 1990 and 2019, the share of households headed by a single woman leapfrogged from 17.6% to 22.6%. (Coauthor Steve notes that even the 1990 figure would have been unthinkable when he was growing up in 1950s rural Idaho.) When it comes to married households, women are heads of household in 46.1% of families. In America's black communities, fully 52.5% are run by a woman. And if you don't consider marital status, roughly half of all households in the United States are woman-led.

Now onto the causes of the shift. Again, the massive changes to America's domestic structure largely stem from four major disrupters that hit post-war America. Yet unlike a "one-two" punch combo in a boxing ring, the forces attacking the traditional American family didn't cease punching when masculinity fell to the canvas. They kept on coming. Here they are.

Disruptor One: Free Love

What comes to mind when you consider the Free Love Movement? It might be The Beatles singing, "Why Don't We Do It in the road?" It might be bra burning. From an altogether different vantage point, it might be a loss of innocence and men taking advantage of young women.

These examples possess a 1960s hippie feel. In truth, the modern Free Love Movement possesses roots in the 1940s. As far back as the World War II years, so-called sexual liberation was about doing whatever you wanted, whenever you wanted, with whomever you wanted. Traditional appeals to morality at this time were to be ignored, or at least discounted. And all this sinful behavior was sanctioned via a veneer of respectability—thanks to pseudo-science cooked up by the likes of sexologist Dr. Alfred Charles Kinsey (of The Kinsey Scale fame).

As PBS explains, the concept of Free Love began before the '60s, largely due to the Bohemian and Beat movements that sprang up before the first longhair arrived shoeless in

San Francisco's Haight-Ashbury District. Free love, including homosexuality, was a "sign of bravado" to the community. It also benefitted far-left sensibilities because it went against traditional familial arrangements.

Another major driver for the Free Love Movement was the approval of the birth control pill ("The Pill") in 1960, influencing people's changing attitudes about (casual) sex. The Supreme Court ruled in 1965, in *Griswold v. Connecticut*, that states could not make The Pill illegal for married women, allowing extant cultural disruption to blast off like a rocket. In response, some tried to sound alarms about The Pill. Consider author Pearl Buck's words in *Reader's Digest*: "Everyone knows what The Pill is. It is a small object—yet its potential effect upon our society many be even more devastating than the nuclear bomb."

Disruptor Two: Feminism

If The Pill enabled free love to take hold by divorcing sex from future responsibility, it also led to feminism's rise. Mona Charen documented how this ideology introduced instability into the American family in a 2018 piece for the *New York Post*.

Charen wrote:

> In 1970, three furious feminist tracts dominated the bestseller lists: Kate Millett's *Sexual Politics*, Germaine Greer's *The Female Eunuch*, and Shulamith Firestone's *The Dialectic of Sex*. They, and others who comprised what was then called the "women's lib" movement, fulminated against male dominance, endorsed sexual liberation, and demanded that the nuclear family be smashed.
>
> . . .

In 2012, Katie Roiphe, feminist and mother of two children by different fathers, condemned concerns about single motherhood: "If there is anything that currently oppresses the children, it is the idea of the way families are 'supposed to be.'" That's the feminist mantra, but "alternative" families work only for a tiny minority. For most women, children and, as we're coming to understand better with each passing year, men, the traditional family remains the gold standard.

So, feminism, under the guise of "liberating" women, instead trapped them in unhappy careers and single-parent households. This resulted in insecure and confused kids—and a repetition of the deleterious cycle. That's not the only harm produced by feminism, which by its nature, radicalizes more people with each passing generation. Modern "third-wave" feminism now promotes the idea that men and women are *exactly the same* except for their genitals, ignoring basic truths. If you've ever wondered why biological males like Lia Thomas can now compete against women in sports like swimming, smashing records for women's events, you can thank your local feminist.

Disruptor Three: The War on Men

Not content with merely changing mothers into hard-nosed career women, feminists and others intent on breaking down the traditional family next turned their sights to men. Wishing to degrade and diminish males' already waning cultural influence, these individuals coined a new epithet to condemn men, an evocative term that's since gone viral—*toxic masculinity.*

The concept of toxic masculinity, labeling alpha male behaviors as bad while rewarding timidity and feminized male behaviors, began amongst feminist intelligentsia. It's since gone mainstream. Incredibly, the American Psychological Association (APA) now recognizes toxic masculinity as a malady, stating: "Traditional masculinity is psychologically harmful, and causes damage that echoes both inwardly and outwardly." Also, according to the APA, masculinity "has been shown to limit males' psychological development, constrain their behavior, resulting in gender role strain and gender role conflict and negatively influence mental health and physical health."

Unsurprisingly, modern feminist doctrine rewards other forms of (dubious) male conduct. Such behaviors include beta/gamma male actions, like celebrating sterilization, meekly obeying rules no matter how asinine, and condoning sexual liaisons outside a committed partnership. To this point, Canadian psychologist, professor, and author Jordan Peterson believes the toxic masculinity label is an attempt to eradicate maleness from our culture altogether, creating a *neutered male* to replace the alpha. But as Peterson cautions: "There are biological differences between men and women that express themselves in temperament and in occupational choice. Any attempt to enforce equality of outcomes is unwarranted and ill-advised as a consequence."

Disruptor Four: The Cult of Narcissism

Legendary football coach Lou Holtz was once asked what's wrong with modern culture. He replied: "The push to a narcissistic society; we have gone from a society of responsibilities to a society of rights and privileges." If you wonder what he meant by that, just observe young people around you, especially how their online behavior is driven to neurotic degrees by a burning desire to receive "likes" and "shares," even from strangers on social media.

Dr. Jim Taylor, psychologist and parenting expert writing for *HuffPost*, points out that our culture is becoming narcissistic at a breathless pace. He documents a study showing the number of young people classified as such by personality tests has doubled in the last 30 years. Meanwhile, the flip side of narcissism—caring for others—is declining. Empathy has also fallen by 40% since 1980.

It's no secret that today's prevalence of narcissism is largely driven by social media peer pressure and a pop culture obsessed with vapid celebrities. Think about your childhood. Do you recall people being "famous for being famous?" These days, the Kardashians make more money than the GDP (gross domestic product) of small countries without an ounce of talent in the family. Interestingly and along the same lines, Taylor demonstrates that a study of lyrics in popular music shows an increase in narcissistic material—for instance, a rise of songs dominated by words like "I" and "me"—instead of empathic words like "we" and "us." Modern lyrics also demonstrate increased hostility over happy emotions. (This study considered the fact that rap music is often violent in tone and self-aggrandizing, but the shift is rampant across all music genres.)

THE FOUR DISRUPTORS HAVE DISTORTED THE SOCIAL IMAGINARY

One final note. Have you ever watched an old movie with an element that seems crazy by today's standards? Maybe it's a film with a hospital scene where patients smoke cigarettes in bed and/or a doctor who lights up during surgery. When young people see this kind of cinematic fare, they are left mouth agape, asking, "*Um, how could anyone have been okay with this?*"

They can't imagine such behavior because it doesn't fit with their *social imaginary*. Philosopher Charles Taylor coined this term to describe rules both written and unwritten dictating how we perceive and act within a culture. According to Taylor, the social imaginary is "how people fit together with others, how things go on between them and their fellows, the expectations that are normally met, and the deeper normative notions and images that underlie these expectations."

The four disruptions have altered our social imaginary about *men*. How most of the population now thinks about masculinity has so radically shifted since World War II it would be hardly recognizable to a 19th century person. This change has come at tremendous cost—not only for individual men left insecure and playing roles instead of living genuine lives, but also for society. Our culture now suffers from lack of strong masculinity in a thousand different ways. Fortunately, just as there are four disruptors at the heart of the crisis, an association of four committed men can help us escape it.

But change won't be easy. In our next chapter, we will examine in more detail the costs of our crisis and how Power of 4 can turn things around.

But first . . .

YOUR PROBLEM: POWER OF 4'S SOLUTION

So far, we have discussed macro trends affecting men, contributing to the malaise, anxiety, and overall diminished quality of life for our sex. Now, we would like to go micro. We wish to drill down and explain how Power of 4 can offer practical solutions for universal challenges we presently face.

In short, our group (and yours too, should you choose to join and/or start one) can help men deal with daily life.

Specifically, that means we are here to support one another.

If you think about this fallen world as a kind of sewer, our job every day is to stay out of the filth. What makes this hard is that the grime is *alluring*. It's easy to be tempted by any number of sins: lust, drugs, alcohol, pride, etc. We help our brothers stay out of the sewer, so we have a better perspective on the big picture. But we also know it's quite easy to slip back. The sewer's pull never really goes away and so each session is a chance to soften our hearts to our families and friends, yet also harden them against temptation, doubt, and fear.

In Part I, we will discuss the challenges we presently face and the need for our brotherhood. Part II will show you what this brotherhood is like in action, offering real-life stories about how Power of 4 helped the brothers navigate their challenges. Part III will offer best practices, giving you the practical tools to get going today.

Let's return to our story now.

CHAPTER 2

I Am Involved in Mankind

There are many sayings we use on a regular basis that we either misattribute or have no clue who first said them. One phrase critical to Power of 4 is: "No man is an island." If you conducted a poll of your friends, the most common guesses would likely be that this famous phrase comes from the Bible or that reliable quote machine, William Shakespeare. Both are incorrect. The expression originates from the famous English poet John Donne.

How Donne brought us this eternal wisdom is more surprising. But first, on the rare occasion someone *does* know the words belong to Donne, they're still usually unable to name which poem they came from. That's because the poet didn't say the famous phrase in his usual medium. A man of the cloth, Donne said them in a sermon delivered in St. Paul's Cathedral in 1642.

To appreciate Donne's words, we must share them in context. His sermon reads:

> No man is an island entire of itself; every man is a piece of the continent, a part of the main; if a clod be washed away by the sea, Europe is the less, as well as if a promontory were, as well as any manner of thy friends or of thine own were; any man's death

diminishes me, because I am involved in mankind. And therefore never send to know for whom the bell tolls; it tolls for thee.

Turns out this sermon is sort of a "two for one" in the famous phrases department. (Although the line "for whom the bell tolls" is mainly associated with novelist Ernest Hemingway!) Returning to Donne, what *does* all that pretty talk about islands and continents mean? Power of 4 understands his point to be that all men share a brotherhood, a fraternity of unique masculine traits enabling them to walk God's path towards a purposeful life. Should this comradery break—should men become islands to themselves—they would be set adrift in a way that diminishes *other* men.

As Donne says, we are all "involved in mankind." This insight dovetails with chapter one's theme. It also puts the problem facing men in clearer terms. Once more, the four disruptors we discussed have one particularly negative effect: Isolating men.

As a reminder, they are:

* Disruptor One: The Sexual Revolution

* Disruptor Two: Feminism's Ascendancy

* Disruptor Three: The War on Men

* Disruptor Four: Society's Casual Embrace of Narcissism

As we saw in the last chapter, these bad societal forces work in concert, forcing men to play roles instead of being "real people." It should also come as no surprise that when we inhabit parts like actors, instead of embracing masculinity inherent to our gender, we become unmoored. Unhappy.

Adrift. When this occurs, we are left feeling as isolated as the figurative island Donne described 300 years before World War II.

LOST

Of course, when we share this idea with other men, they're likely to reply, "But I have *lots* of friends. How can you say I'm isolated?" The trouble is that feelings of isolation can manifest differently from person to person. Example: If you've amassed a big group of buddies, enjoy a successful career and family, but still feel depressed, you're most likely isolated.

Ironically, men raised in our narcissistic era understand the isolation concept better than their forebears. Ask a youngster active on social media how they feel when their "friends" (2,000 strong) reply to their fun posts (what they ate for breakfast; their vacation photos) yet say nothing when asked for real emotional support. (Think: the time they posted about losing a loved one.)

This is isolation in action.

Of course, the real isolation isn't from *others*. It's from masculinity, God, and, of course, *yourself.* When men must play roles that constantly shift due to culture's fickle demands, the workplace, and/or family life, we are isolated from the purpose God laid out for us. We are isolated from the masculinity hard-wired into our brains. We are isolated from ourselves. Donne saw this danger hundreds of years ago. Now, it's up to us in the modern age to reverse the trend. How might we do it? Power of 4's answer is "with the help of God and three friends." But before we get into that, let's talk about one path that will never lead you back to where God wants you—western philosophy.

GREAT THINKERS. BAD OUTCOMES.

Even if you know little to nothing about modern philosophy, you've doubtless heard the names of famous philosophers. Western culture holds them in highest esteem as the smart guys who "figured it all out." Thanks to their sagacious wisdom, we're "better people."

There's just one problem with this idea.

Many philosophers generated ideas that gnawed away at Christianity, traditional culture, and most importantly for this book, eroded notions of masculinity. Bruce, one of our brothers, had his eyes opened on this topic at the last place you might expect—a going-away party for a work colleague.

Here's the story as he tells it:

> My associate of many years was retiring with plans to start his own business. He was a great guy, older than me, and always kind. A Christian who never mistreated his subordinates, he was good at his job, too. We threw a goodbye celebration for him, and after everyone had a few drinks and ties were loosened, he gave us an impromptu lesson on his contempt for those philosophers who shaped modern thinking.
>
> Now, I didn't study philosophy much in school. I kept my head in practical subjects and looked to the Lord for guidance on other matters. But my retiring buddy, Chris, knew his stuff and started a round robin discussion on how so many intellectuals really messed us up.
>
> Taking in the diverse group of coworkers at the party, he confidently said, "Name any philosopher and I'll tell you how they've helped turn modern

society upside down. And no cheating by naming a Christian thinker like C.S. Lewis."

A woman named Barbara took the bait. "What about Sartre? I love his books."

Chris didn't skip a beat. "Jean-Paul Sartre was an atheist who taught that the world existence proceeds essence. He believed you aren't a soul. *You're a bag of meat.* By convincing people there's no essential human nature—that God didn't define manhood or womanhood—Sartre makes it easy to argue pretty much any bad behavior is just fine."

The group was taken aback by Chris's seriousness. I think they expected a joke. But a moment later Bill from accounting raised his hand like we were in school. "Okay, what about Darwin?"

Chris snorted. "Darwin's too easy. By convincing the world via the theory of evolution that humans evolved from monkeys, he broke an essential link between God the creator and humankind. Also, Social Darwinism or 'survival of the fittest' became an excuse for nearly every nasty act of the 20th century."

Chris, picking up steam, surveyed the group: "Next."

Another woman asked, "How about Sigmund Freud? Hasn't the father of psychoanalysis been a positive for mankind?"

Chris replied without hesitation. "Don't I wish! Freud emphasized the subconscious mind to such a degree it became a crutch for everything that goes wrong in life. When men go overboard with Freud, every problem becomes the product of their mom or their poor childhood or their subconscious. What ever happened to taking the blame when things go bad? Also, I'll just say that there is practically *no* scientific evidence for any of his theories—like the stages of development or 'penis envy.' Yet they somehow ended up being completely accepted by the psychology academia, just like Darwin in biology."

Although this went on for some time with Chris schooling the room, one final example towered above the others. A coworker named George, perhaps having heard this lecture before, stood up with a grin. "What about B.F. Skinner?"

Recognizing the playful tone in George's voice, Chris replied at once. "Ah, I was wondering when someone would mention the great behavioralist. Skinner developed operant conditioning in the 1920s. He believed humans have no internal guidance and no conscience, so it's up to the powers-that-be to give us the right stimuli to ensure the proper outcomes. Skinner takes away the agency God gave us. In his mind, we don't do things because they are "good." We do them because the "good" lever offers us a piece of cheese while the "bad" lever delivers an electric shock. Thanks to Skinner, our workplaces and schools treat us like rats in a maze instead of God's children. So that's a big 'no thank you, Skinner' from me."

As someone who didn't know much about philosophers at the time, I stood speechless. Chris was saying all these great minds didn't have the best interest of men or God at heart. Quite the opposite. Using trickery and other mental feats, they wished to isolate and reshape us into the people they wanted us to be—but who gave them that right?

WHAT BEING AN ISLAND DOES TO A MAN

Once more, the four disruptors and a hundred years of western philosophy have isolated men from ourselves, our innate masculinity, and God's path. Obviously, this is bad. How bad? To begin with, it's messing up our minds. According to the National Center for Health Statistics (NCHS), one in ten American men suffer from depression. Of those who self-report feeling this way, less than half sought professional treatment.

This figure is terrible enough, amounting to millions of Americans, but it likely hides the problem's true scope. Many depressed men are loathe to admit such feelings, and perhaps an even larger number don't even know they are depressed. Some male sufferers may think it's normal to have no desire to get out of bed, to face their day. Others may cling to the mistaken idea that they should "tough it out," unwilling to admit to themselves or others the ugly truth.

Along the same lines and according to a survey by the *Today* show of 1,000 American men, 49% of respondents have felt more depressed than they admitted to family and friends. To many males, mental illness and suicidal thoughts are shameful or embarrassing. As a result, they suffer alone instead of turning to a support network. These men are the islands Donne described.

Of course, men that aren't willing to seek help often self-medicate. This can take helpful forms like hitting the gym daily, but it's more likely to surface in bad ways, like abusing alcohol and drugs. The Centers for Disease Control and Prevention's (CDC) stats on the former are startling. Men are twice as likely to binge-drink than women. Anyone who has been around this behavior knows it's when people make stupid (and sometimes deadly) decisions. Men are also almost twice as likely to be alcoholics than women. In fact, men account for 75% of all alcohol-related deaths annually.

But, abusing drugs and alcohol isn't the worst possible outcome. Suicide takes that distinction. Men left adrift are in pain. Some of this suffering comes from trauma, which the V.A. reports impacts the lives of six in ten men, whether from combat, workplace accidents, or other sources. And sometimes this pain results in the ultimate tragedy of taking one's own life. Although women kill themselves too, suicide is a more pressing concern for men. CDC data shows men kill themselves almost *four times* as often.

Worse, suicide data is even more grim when you examine it for disparate age groups. Most heartbreakingly, suicide rates have skyrocketed amongst the young. According to the CDC, for Americans ages 10–24, suicide is the third-leading cause of death. For 10- to 14-year-old preteens and "tweens," it's the second-leading. Anyone familiar with the stresses kids have experienced during the COVID pandemic knows these stats are likely to increase, not decrease. Many youngsters ended their lives before they even had a chance to find their paths.

Naturally, suicide's incidence is quite high among those nearing their path's end. The APA reports the group with the highest numbers of suicides in America is white men over age 85. Their rate is an astounding *four times higher* than the rest of the population. Those men who should be passing wisdom on to their descendants are instead taking it to their grave, an undeniable calamity worthy of our prayers.

Bad as this is, suicide is just one of *many* problems produced by a society that has split men from masculinity. Uncovering the reasons why we are in this place and the bad effects it has produced is critical to understanding Power of 4's mission: to rebuild men. We get there by being genuine people again, embracing our masculinity, and living with God's purpose. Nothing could be more important. It's literally a matter of life or death.

Now it's time to change our focus from the big picture to the details within it, beginning with another story about Mark.

MARK EXPLAINS HOW HE ONCE PLAYED A ROLE

When we men play roles, our focus centers on what we are *doing*, not who we are *being*. This is instantly recognizable to any man who has been at a party recently or even sat beside a stranger on a plane. The universal first question you receive in either situation goes like this: "So, what do you do?"

Why is this the male go-to ice breaker at social occasions? Simple. Think about it like this: What matters most to an actor is the role they are playing, not the person they are. Accordingly, us men who are stuck playing roles derive our sense of identity by what we do, and little else.

After all, too many of us men don't talk about our feelings or our thoughts. Instead, we yap about our career aspirations—or worse, how much money we make—as if these things somehow define the human experience. This fact of life is especially pronounced in a society that still expects men to play economic roles, like provider, protector, and source of financial support.

This was the scenario at the party described in chapter one, when Steve met Mark and the first seeds of Power of 4 were sown. Also, you'll recall Mark's joke about Haddie the dog and the kids who were really disturbed to learn that their dog had passed, not their dad. Mark told the joke to get a laugh and bring some levity to the gathering, but inside, he felt like *he* was the father in the tale. To expand on why he felt this way at the time, Mark offers this sketch of his life nearly 20 years ago.

Mark's Life Was the Road

Back then Mark traveled 200+ days annually as he threw his energy into launching an investment firm spanning the West Coast. Based on the numbers, he was doing a fine job fulfilling the provider role, but he was unhappy at home. For all his income and status as a corporate leader, he felt inadequate. The source of his grief concerned a fundamental disconnect from who he was and the role he played in the world. Mark sometimes felt more connected to his business peers than to his own family. "I was so isolated back then," Mark confessed. "And didn't know it."

Mark's View of His Marriage

According to Mark—and his coauthor—he married out of his league. Margy is a kind, patient, Christian woman with a strong belief in her vows. She's also the glue that keeps their family together. Long ago, Mark made Margy a promise that she always expected him to follow: "I'll put everything that matters first, then the business second—I'll never miss a birthday."

What Worked Well in Their Marriage

Though Mark put in long hours, he kept his promise. In his view, he and his wife were at their closest when they worked to support a better future together. Long before calendars were an app on smartphones, Mark and Margy would sit down with dual calendars to plot Mark's travel and family events. This way Margy knew where he was daily, and Mark knew when to expect the next lacrosse tournament (he coached). Margy also supported Mark by making sure he didn't miss little details, like putting cash in his wallet to tip the taxi driver after an airport trip. They ran things as a true partnership with the mutual goal of financial success.

Of course, it wasn't all smooth sailing. Margy sometimes had to crack the whip to keep Mark's priorities straight. Mark describes himself as a "loose cannon" during this time, accepting projects with little regard for what it meant to his workload, not to mention his family. "I was the kind of guy who'd take a business call from the delivery room, hitting mute 'til the baby came out." It's no surprise Margy had to help Mark set rules about traveling. If not, he might have spent even *more* time on the road. Yet from Mark's perspective, this was the lifestyle required to get ahead, or the next shark might swim faster than him and snatch the deal.

WHAT DIDN'T WORK
IN THEIR EARLY MARRIAGE

Reflecting on this period, Mark gives us an unvarnished view. He knows what he could have done better. Topping the list is an obvious one. He was too focused on competing in business. "Margy could almost see the deals rolling around in my head, whether we were on a date night, watching the kids play sports—even at church."

At the same time, Mark struggled to show empathy towards her. "I would sometimes treat Margy like a client I had to close. I would lay out my suggestions, then expect her to put them in place without another thought. But this was crazy and not helpful, especially since I spent more time in hotels than in our house some months."

Mark can admit now that he thought he was the most critical part of their relationship. Also, that it was Margy's duty to support him. He wasn't nearly as concerned with how he might support her—beyond financial support. "Back then I thought of myself much more than I thought of her. I justified this feeling through my vaunted role as breadwinner." All these issues were swirling in Mark's life before Power of 4.

And he faced even more problems in corporate America.

HOW OUR DISRUPTORS MESSED UP THE WORKPLACE—ESPECIALLY FOR MEN

When men struggle with something hard, the advice they often get is to "man up." In corporate America, this translates to "get the job done, but do it . . . like a woman." (You may have felt the same thing in your own career, even if you haven't exactly heard it put this way before.) Why is this?

Decades of feminism and propaganda about "toxic masculinity" have produced workplaces that expect males to lead like women. This emphasis on feminine leadership, where telling employees what to do is seen as "chauvinistic"—and men are expected to chat with subordinates about their feelings—is a hard environment for a man with any degree of masculinity to perform in. It turns out such workplaces are bad for *everyone,* as documented in the *Harvard Business Review* in an article entitled, "How Men Get Penalized for Straying from Masculine Norms," by David M. Mayer.

Mayer writes the following on "being nicer":

> Given that many of us want more nice guys at work, we might assume that men would be celebrated for being calm and unassuming. Wrong. Research has found that men who are more communal and agreeable (e.g., warm, caring, supportive, sympathetic) made significantly less money than more stereotypically masculine men. More agreeable men across multiple industries made an average of 18% less in

income and were evaluated as less likely to have management potential as compared to less agreeable men.

Similarly, "nice guys" were evaluated as less competent and less hirable for managerial roles. One experimental study found that male managers in consulting who tended to advocate more for their team than for themselves were judged to be lower in agency and competence and more likely to be considered for job dismissal. Unfortunately, given the costs— real and psychological—of being a nice guy at work, men may be less likely to engage in these behaviors that could help their own career and make them better colleagues.

Mayer has this to say about considering others' feelings:

Empathy is an important part of leadership. However, women are more likely to receive "credit" for it than men. A recent study found that female leaders who displayed empathy (as reported by their employees) were less likely to be in danger of career derailment—e.g., problems with interpersonal relationships, difficulty building and leading teams, difficulty changing and adapting, failure in meeting business goals and objectives, and having too narrow a functional orientation. Men did not get this boost—there was no relationship between male leaders' empathy and their bosses' assessment of potential career derailment. These findings are consequential because displaying empathy is critical for leading effectively.

Extrapolating from Meyers' words, let's return to Mark's situation. For years, men like him found themselves in a

Catch-22. Expected to go against their masculine nature, they were punished by corporate culture for *doing what they were asked to do*. Still, despite feeling pressure to be a female-style boss, Mark stayed true to his masculine nature. He steadfastly believed that if he slowed down, even for a second, someone else might eat his lunch.

WOMEN SUFFER FROM PLAYING A ROLE IN CORPORATE AMERICA TOO

Even before men were pressured to feminize their ways in business, women were also forced to adjust their work style. By emulating men. In Mark's view, corporate women tried to be "Superwomen," juggling both corporate and family responsibilities.

In fact, juggling became the pastime for both sexes after World War II. Just as women were expected to straddle two identities—to keep those plates forever spinning—so did men. Males that were supposed to bring home the bacon were now expected to be modern, *nurturing* husbands. Such nurturing often meant staying home like Michael Keaton in *Mr. Mom*, supporting the wife's career.

This development blurred the sexes' responsibilities, creating androgyny whereby men and women played interchangeable roles in the family and workplace dynamics. This unusual situation extended beyond the corporate world, reaching into the church. Steve recalls his experience taking a class titled "Women in Ministry" decades ago. "Even then, the entire focus of the course was on *gender*, not on performance," he recalls.

In other words, the professor and students mostly cared about getting more women into ministry, not about molding students into strong ministers. The only man present, Steve wondered how the group could possibly have a balanced discussion on any subject. "As I recall, the answer to nearly every question was: 'Men don't respect women in the ministry,' leading me to constantly raise my hand and ask, 'Are you considering the personality differences between the sexes?'"

To a group obsessed with androgyny, his query made as much sense as if he had spoken in tongues. Given all these societal pressures, is it any surprise men like Mark and Steve have long felt isolated because they can't keep up with the ground shifting beneath their feet? Does it ever feel this way to you? We men are told the role we play is bad. Then we are told we must change our role. If and when we finally do, we are then told we are playing the new role badly.

WHAT THE BIBLE SAYS ABOUT MEN AND WOMEN

The Bible tells us there is a clear division between the sexes, though both genders are important. As St. Paul's first letter to the Corinthians explains: "However, in the Lord, neither is woman independent of man, nor is man independent of woman. (1 Corinthians 11:11, New American Standard Bible [NASB])" What won't you find in the Bible? A single word endorsing an androgynous mixing of gender roles (at home or work) as promoted by modern thinking.

Thankfully, the Bible has guided Power of 4's formation in a major way. Have you ever stopped to ponder who Jesus chose as His disciples? The twelve apostles came from varied backgrounds, but all were men. And although He chose a dozen, He spent the most time with just three. In essence, Jesus ran the first Power of 4 group. If He chose to live out His faith with three brothers, today's man would do well to take the same approach—some 2,000 years later.

ENTER POWER OF 4

Mark's career struggles were the perfect topic for the first Power of 4 meeting, held just over 18 years ago as of this writing. The group back then consisted of Steve and Mark—who are still in it today, along with Andrew and Bruce, who later both moved from the area. Not long after the Haddie story kicked things off, they met at Steve's office at 6:30 a.m. to ensure privacy. (Steve had some prior experience, as he had been in a different men's group years earlier, but the others did not.)

Still, any awkwardness melted away as soon as Mark described his dilemma. "I have the biggest opportunity of my career on the table. I've been offered the Head of Sales position but I'm unsure if I should take it. I'd be on the road an extra 50 days a year and be relocated to Boston. I gotta tell you, I'm really struggling with being unsure about this because, in my mind, I'm made of stronger stuff. This *should* be a no-brainer, but it just isn't."

Steve, with the heart of a counselor but the pragmatic mind of a C-suite executive, wished to translate Mark's feelings into tangible data points. He began with pros and cons of the position. "Mark, let's start with the good stuff. Why should you take this job?"

"The compensation package would be huge. I'd get an immediate salary bump, a better bonus, and over time I could potentially triple my income."

Andrew, who was a mid-level manager making a respectable income, cut in. "Mark, what's to think about here? You're talking life-changing numbers."

"I agree, but I'm *already* away from my family 150 nights a year. Raising that up to 200 makes me wonder . . . will my kids even recognize me when I get home from the airport?"

As Andrew nodded in understanding, Mark continued, "But this job goes beyond money, if I'm being honest. I'd have an important title that would make people notice me in the industry. I'd have more responsibility and authority than I've ever had. I've always wanted to be in the 'big boys club,' and look, the 'big boys club' *is now on the table.*"

Bruce chimed in. "Okay. Let's go back to cons. So, the travel seems bad, what else is giving you second thoughts?"

Mark let his concerns pour out, feeling validated by the group as they hung on his every word. "The weather's terrible. Can you imagine a Boston winter after Southern California? I'd also lose surfing—"

"Which I credit with keeping Mark sane," Steve put in.

Mark had to smile. "He's right. That *is* my outlet. Plus, my family would be uprooted, causing all sorts of problems for Margy, who is caring for her mother, and, of course, my kids who are just starting school."

Steve asked, "What does Margy think?"

"She's amazingly supportive. She'd follow me anywhere. She told me it's up to me to make this decision for the family."

Yet even as he said this, Mark felt the urge to lay it all out in the open. "Part of me feels ready for this, but another part is screaming that moving across the country for this is a mistake, that it's not who I am or who I want to be." Mark was more surprised at his vulnerable admission than his brothers. They reacted to his situation without judgment, helping him to gain perspective. They came from different backgrounds with different histories, but each could relate.

At the end of the hour, Mark had made his decision. He wouldn't take it.

Almost two decades later, he reflects on what happened that day. "It may have been our inaugural meeting, but it felt like we had been doing this for years—it was so natural and comfortable. For the first time ever, I had a sounding board of like-minded men who wouldn't cut my throat if it meant they could beat me to a deal. These men helped me understand my personality better than I ever could on my own. I'm an avoider; I fill up my hours to evade emptiness. Their perspectives helped me understand my weakness."

He continues, "The group also helped me realize I could build a better business for myself in innovative ways without the promotion. I expanded our offices, brought in help at the managerial level, and reduced time on the road. Before long, I was managing my work and my *life* better—thanks to their input and support. My single biggest takeaway from Power of 4 is that I was in danger of replacing my role as husband and father by overemphasizing my role as provider. No one should become a paycheck with legs."

What Mark desperately needed was a mirror to see what was *really* happening to him, his family, and his career. Power of 4 did this by giving him space to unpack his situation and find his own answers. (Note: No one told him what to do. And no one brought up his childhood.) Power of 4 also gave him a key insight we must remember—even in our darkest hours. Modern life's many confusions can be reduced when men can (finally) be open, honest, and vulnerable with other men in a private and protected space. What we term "coming ugly."

Mark made a leap of faith to "come ugly" to Power of 4 that day, and it paid off. It can pay off for you too! In chapter three, we'll examine how materialism's pursuit has left so many men in a plight like Mark's, and how to fix it.

CHAPTER 3

Your Life is Our Agenda

Our first two chapters began with stories directly involving the authors. Now we want to discuss a different narrative from the ancient past—a tale so old it was still ancient—even when coauthor Steve was a little boy. We're going all the way back to the beginning: to the Garden of Eden. Practically everyone knows at least a little bit about Adam and Eve. The typical level of understanding goes something like this: "Eve ate the forbidden fruit at the snake's suggestion, convincing Adam to eat it too . . . bada-boom, bada-bing, they were cast out of the Garden of Eden."

Even some Christians are happy with this surface-level explanation. But to really understand modern man's plight, we must come to terms with the quandary of the *first man*. Now, you may wonder what your life shares with Adam, who the Bible says lived about 6,000 years ago—especially when you don't feel like you have much in common with your male ancestors from just one or two generations back.

Yet, when you learn more about this story, you just might be surprised.

WHAT ADAM CAN
TEACH US ABOUT OURSELVES

Adam lived to be almost 1,000 years old. The financially savvy reader may be interested in his activities late in his life (He must have had a fantastic retirement plan to fund that kind of lifespan, right?), but we're more interested in his early days dwelling in the Garden of Eden. Even so, one of the first things we're bound to hear when we mention Adam, especially from young men, is: "Um. Why should I care?"

The short answer is because Jesus and His Apostles *cared*. C. John Collins, professor of Old Testament at Covenant Theological Seminary in St. Louis, explains in an essay for *The Gospel Coalition* that, "The main apostolic passage reflecting on [Adam and Eve] comes in Romans 5:12–21. Some would tell us that Paul is the only apostle to make much of the story, but they are mistaken; in Matthew's Gospel Jesus himself bases an argument on it."

If Jesus cared, we must care. So, what can we learn? According to the Book of Genesis, Chapter 2, God created humankind "after his image." First, He made Adam from dust and later fashioned Eve, as his companion, from Adam's rib. Although the Garden of Eden functioned as a "paradise on earth," these first humans were not afforded lives of luxury. In fact, God assigned them two important jobs. First, Adam was given dominion over all beasts and plants to act as steward. Second, Adam and Eve were tasked with populating earth.

Content in their roles, the first man and woman lived a charmed existence. They also had two characteristics that made them special. Notably, Adam and Eve possessed free will. God did not create humans to be puppets. He wanted humanity to *choose* to worship Him and obey His rules. Which Adam and Eve did. For a time.

Next, these first humans were born without sin. They walked around naked without even the strategic fig leaves furnished by so many later artists. This is because no shame existed back then. Of course, just one look at the sinful world we all inhabit makes it clear this pristine state did not last long.

Its demise can be attributed to the simple prohibition God gave Adam:

> The LORD God commanded the man, saying, "From any tree of the garden you may freely eat; but from the tree of the knowledge of good and evil you shall not eat, for on the day that you eat from it you will certainly die. (Genesis 2:16-17, NASB)"

What happened next is familiar to most people, Christian or not. Satan, in the form of a serpent, tricked Eve into eating forbidden fruit. Interestingly, we know this fruit as an apple, but it wasn't any apple we know today. The reference website Answers in Genesis explains the mix-up is due to the Latin translation of the Old Testament, which does indeed use the word for apple. (The original Hebrew text employs a completely different word for the fruit, which is otherwise only described as being seedless.)

Regardless of the actual fruit, modern man's real troubles began with what happened after Eve took that first bite. Once Eve broke God's rule, she had little trouble convincing Adam to do the same. They instantly regretted their decision as they changed the course of their lives and indeed all of humanity. They soon felt shame toward their nakedness. But the shame was only about to start piling up.

You see, when God confronted Adam about his sin, Adam did something all too usual. He passed the buck! Adam blamed Eve for convincing him to eat the forbidden fruit. Eve, in turn, blamed the serpent. (We've ruminated within our group over the years if part of Adam's problem was that he was the only man around. What if he had a Power of 4 to hash out what Eve did? The world might have turned out very different.)

Speculations aside, we know how this tragedy ended. God expelled Adam and Eve from Eden for all time, and sin was set loose on the world. The rest of Genesis shows how badly Adam erred. Events in his lifetime could have been ripped from today's headlines. Murder. Turning away from God. Bigamy. Far more calamitous, his sin was passed down to all future humans, including you and the authors of this book. It's a concept that's easy to forget although it was once clearly understood by every child in America.

Turning to scholar John Collins again, he explains that *The New England Primer* used to be standard educational text. The book even includes rhyming lines to help kids learn their ABCs. The one for "A," in the 1777 edition, includes a phrase we should all keep in mind: "In Adam's fall, we sinned all."

This understanding of how sin intruded into God's world, leaving humanity estranged from their creator, is why this story matters today.

It may be hard to admit, but we are all fallen creatures. Due to Adam and Eve, we all share in iniquity and imperfection. It's easy to see this manifested in the problems and evils surrounding us, but harder to admit to ourselves. It gets a bit easier in a Power of 4—but only if in our hearts we accept the truth. We are fallen, but Jesus came to earth to redeem us, and in pursuing our redemption, we have obligations to each other. In particular, men are to be the head of the family as God is the head of mankind.

THE TRUE MEANING OF "COME UGLY"

You may have noticed we haven't completely defined what "come ugly" means in the context of Power of 4. We couldn't explain it without first documenting Adam's fall. *Come ugly* is the first commandment of Power of 4. We let our faults show. We don't disguise our warts, our mistakes, or our foibles. Hiding those things is a big part of modern life, but it will never serve you well.

We'll give you a related, modern counterexample. If you know a young man who uses online dating services, you probably have heard horror stories about women who look nothing like their pictures, thanks to filters and image manipulation. In past generations, a similar (analog) artifice might have occurred if a gal was adept at applying makeup. But don't fool yourself for a second in thinking only women take part in such disguises.

Men do the same thing in different ways. Many of us hide our faults by buying that expensive car, even when it's out of our price range. We wear fancy clothes to cover up insecurities. We show the world an idealized version of ourselves, what we think others want to see. But behaving in this false manner never results in personal growth or coming closer to God's design. To do that, we must recognize our faults and be honest with our brothers.

Accordingly, within Power of 4, we stress unvarnished honesty. Knowing we're sinners, there's no point in pretending to be the most pious in the room. The group has even built a collection of sayings to reinforce coming ugly. For example, "Men who are vulnerable with other men stop wasting energy preparing to defend themselves. Instead, they channel it toward living on purpose." What's more, Power of 4 recognizes that when men come ugly, they improve themselves while improving others. We like to say, "A man who listens to another man's confessions, and then confesses his own failures, is building humility into his character."

By coming to Power of 4 without pretense, without papering over life's problems, without adding a veneer of perfection, we acknowledge that we all have problems. Yet working together, we can tackle them. Mark realized this truth in his earliest days with the group.

WHEN MARK FELT
LOCKED OUT OF THE GARDEN

Let's consider the predicament Mark faced before that first Power of 4 meeting from chapter two. Why did conflict exist in his life? Why did he respond to Steve's request to join the newly formed group? Mark had attained much success with the promise of even more wealth on the horizon. Still, he knew he lacked something. He was missing God and meaning. He felt much like those first two humans forever locked out of Eden.

The central problem for Mark twenty years ago was that he believed in God and God's design, but his *life* wasn't designed around God's design. Instead, his days were structured, like so many men, around financial success, career goals, and endless competition with others. Those who worked with Mark might have been quick to say about him, "There is none better," but better at *what* exactly?

He wanted to be a better man, not a better vice president. Over the years, Mark built a sterling corporate track record, but he noticed a troubling trend within himself. No matter how much money he earned, he didn't feel fulfilled. An emptiness gnawed at him. And it wouldn't go away. Like many men, more so in our era than ever before, success in his chosen field left him wanting. Although he is modest about his intelligence, Mark was smart enough to evaluate this problem and discern the root cause. His epiphany led him to join Power of 4, seeking the meaning that a bigger office and higher annual revenue couldn't offer.

Importantly, Power of 4 didn't solve this conflict within him. Rather, it gave him the platform to examine his life from 360 degrees. Mark isn't alone in facing this problem. It's become so common we can observe it on a macro level.

FALLEN MEN, FALLEN SOCIETY

Who Moved My Cheese? by Dr. Spencer Johnson is one of the best-selling business books of all time. The joke in Southern California (SoCal) is we can't tell you *who* moved your cheese, but we can tell you *where* it moved to: Orange County, otherwise known as The OC. From all around the world, people flock to The OC to win that proverbial cheese in what they can be forgiven for thinking is a close approximation to the Garden of Eden. The perfect weather, stunning sights, and unimaginable concentration of wealth do seem paradisial, but The OC encapsulates just how far we've fallen from being in touch with God.

In many ways, The OC is the cutting edge of American culture. If you think America has lost its way, The OC can show you how far from a "God First" culture our nation will be in five years. Unfortunately, the land of sun and palm trees embodies the worst values of pop culture, but on steroids. (We should know—nearly all our brothers live here.) The cultural milieu favors acquiring vast wealth without sweating too much to earn it, being a celebrity no matter how ridiculous the reason—or sans any reason—hooking up with others based on perceived status, and winning at all costs, even the expense of personal honor.

Unfortunately, what we see in The OC is a direct result of

Christianity's wane in America. Long gone are the days of *The New England Primer.* According to the Pew Research Center, self-identified Christians make up only 63% of the U.S. population. Does this number seem strong to you? Consider this: Only a decade ago, it was 75%. Christians aren't being replaced by Muslims and Buddhists either—29% of adults say they have no religion whatsoever. Although the survey doesn't extrapolate this far, it's a fair guess the one-third of our population claiming to have no religion worships instead at the altar of materialism, like so many OC denizens.

As we know, materialism puts wealth and worldly goods before everything else, including God. It's a trap many men fall into, but nothing new. The philosopher Sir Francis Bacon said of materialism, "Money is a great servant but a bad master." Thinking along similar lines, novelist Fyodor Dostoevsky writes in *The Brothers Karamazov:* "The world says: 'You have needs—satisfy them. You have as much right as the rich and the mighty. Don't hesitate to satisfy your needs; indeed, expand your needs and demand more.' This is the worldly doctrine of today. And they believe that this is freedom. The result for the rich is isolation and suicide, for the poor, envy and murder."

Long before *The Atlantic* became a mouthpiece for every woke, leftist anti-intellectual, it was a magazine covering important issues. Way back in 1887, it documented the rift between materialism and Christianity, a struggle that has only intensified in our lifetimes. An article entitled "The Growth of Materialism," by author George Frederic Parsons, describes attempts by the church to battle against a shallow philosophy that believes the "incompetent, the idle, and the forceless" should equally share in the "good enjoyed by society."

Parsons wrote:

The church appeals in vain to a generation steeped in materialism, and the more vainly for that it is itself infected with the general taint. Costly church edifices, costly preachers, luxurious surroundings, may and do minister to the thoroughly worldly tastes of those who adhere to nominal religion for conventional and selfish reasons, but they do not and cannot foster spirituality, nor weaken in any degree the hold which Mammon has upon the world. Intellect in the pulpit will always be attractive and may depend upon the kind of appreciation which materialism tenders to all it approves of. It will be paid handsomely. It will be treated deferentially. It will be rewarded with a share of the things which materialism considers most precious and desirable. It will be honored with the social distinctions which flatter the least spiritual tendencies in the sacerdotal nature. So it will become a part of the worldliness its function is to oppose, and a sanction of the ignoble frivolities it should condemn unsparingly. Wealth seduces and neutralizes the church. The spirit of the time broods as heavily upon the altar as upon the desk.

Using deft prose we can scarcely hope to match, Parsons nails the rat race exemplified by The OC. Read his next words carefully and you'll recognize how well they describe the predicament Mark found himself in before the first Power of 4 meeting:

How precious should this gift of riches be, when we consider the extent of the degradation to which the pursuit of it subjects us! Candor and truth, justice and equity, self-respect, and faithfulness, all the qualities which go to make honorable manhood, in short, must be sunk out of sight, done violence to, or perhaps even surrendered altogether, in order to attain the desired end. Putting on the armor of selfishness, we address ourselves to a career which gradually extinguishes the desire for anything better, and of which the most that can be said is that it prepares us in some way for the illusions which crown it.

And this was way back in 1887, when asking someone to Google an address for your GPS would have landed you in the funny farm. What has caused the shift towards materialism in modern culture with increasing velocity? Writing for Creation.com, Clement Butel says the answer is the application of Enlightenment ideals extolled in the 19th century. These were fundamentally anti-faith. Their materialist ideas stated only science can provide answers, paving the way for evolution to be accepted as science fact, denigrating anyone who would deign to challenge this idea.

Butel writes:

In the early post World War II years, evolutionists misused the prestige attached to a genuine scientific achievement (the release of energy in the form of an atomic bomb) to bolster their false claims that organic evolution was not only a genuine scientific theory but also a proven scientific fact.

In the years that followed, the principal causes of the demise of Christian morality as the publicly recognized ethical standard in our society were: (a) propaganda in favor of an evolutionary worldview, (b) the strict censorship in both scientific journals and the popular press against criticism of it, and (c) the white-anting [an Australian term for the erosion of a foundation] of the Christian Churches, not only with 'liberal' ('higher') biblical criticism, but also with acceptance of the evolutionary worldview.

The last-mentioned cause was the most telling because it allowed 'liberals' to replace the Genesis doctrine of Creation with theistic evolution. This removed much of the criticism of evolutionism that otherwise would have been forthcoming from Christian Churches.

Materialism has since overwhelmed pop culture, running roughshod over SoCal. This is partly because it's so profitable for the beneficiaries. If there's nothing more to life than a fancier watch and a bigger house, the companies in those industries make out like bandits—as do their partners. And their partners. But this is also partly because materialism is the easy road to take. It's *easy* to focus on personal pleasure, on feeling good, even if pulling it off requires a prescription for happy pills or some other illicit palliative.

Inevitably, materialism leaves modern man with a nagging question: *"What's missing?"* If you're reading this book, you likely have a firmer basis in faith than the typical guy seeking more cheese in The OC—or anywhere else.

Regardless of your career, financial status, and societal station, you most likely believe in God. Yet, even the most faithful can flounder when navigating the 21st century's complexities. And, if you are being truly honest with yourself, if you are coming ugly, most likely, you wrestle with the same questions we do: *How should faith inform my life? How can I prioritize so many disparate values competing for my attention and concern?*

This internal battle for meaning and purpose was exactly

the struggle faced by Andrew, Power of 4's third original brother. How he broke the spell of materialism and found his true calling is a lesson in faith and following God's design. His inspiring tale is also rooted in another Biblical story. See if you can discern which one as you read ahead.

ANDREW'S DILEMMA: CAREER VS. CALLING

When Power of 4 first formed, Andrew joined right after Steve and Mark. The group came to life before its first meeting with the addition of Bruce. Back then, Andrew thrived as a financial manager living The OC dream as he helped other successful people grow their wealth. Although he showed enthusiasm for the brotherhood from the start, it was obvious Andrew wasn't the sort of guy to come ugly. Andrew was used to wowing clients with signs of his own success, from the flashy car and showy Rolex to the outward appearance of always being calm, cool, and collected.

But inside he was in turmoil. Coming out of that first meeting, where Mark discussed his own dilemma of potential relocation, Andrew realized he might find his way out of his own predicament if he followed suit—if he came ugly for advice.

But before discussing what Andrew told Power of 4, we must set the stage with his backstory. From the time Andrew was born, baseball consumed him. His first memory was swinging a wiffle bat, and he had racked up wins and scholarships as he played his way through college. He parlayed these triumphs into a living centered around his passion. Not good enough for the major leagues, he nonetheless secured a career as a baseball coach at Simpson University, a Christian institution in Northern California (NorCal).

He didn't make much money, though—coaches at

Christian colleges rarely do. However, Andrew enjoyed his job immensely. He also felt he contributed to the world by molding young men into strong competitors with faith in God. So far, so good. But his life was about to take a turn sharper than a Sandy Koufax curveball.

While coaching at Simpson, Andrew was married to his first wife with two young kids. Their marriage fell apart based on many factors, including marrying young. Still, they remained amicable, even sharing custody of the children. But the divorce changed Andrew's life in more ways than one. Years later, he wed his second wife, an ambitious female named Katy. Katy had bigger plans than could be supported by a diminutive baseball coach salary, and she began pushing Andrew towards a career change.

Katy also possessed a savvy mind and recognized Andrew had the brains to do well in the financial world. She saw that SoCal, already a booming economy, was only going to keep booming. She therefore set her sights on The OC, where the best and brightest lived. Going to work on Andrew was the next step. It helped that her man was smitten with her and eager to please. In little time, he felt the lure of wealth himself, instigating his own career plans. He began by taking business classes to sharpen his financial acumen and engaging in networking to build his prospect base.

Before long, Katy's instincts proved correct. For a man immersed in arcane baseball stats, the stock market didn't hold much mystery. Soon Andrew was ready to make the change of a lifetime. Trading in his baseball uniform for a suit, Andrew secured a job in wealth management with a small brokerage, working out of an office near Sunnyvale, but still in NorCal. He quickly moved up the ranks by demonstrating maturity and poise, building an impressive client roster that was as loyal to him as to his brokerage.

It wasn't long before Andrew got his call up to the big leagues. Upon accepting a position down south, Andrew and his family relocated to Newport Beach and took The OC by storm. He ran his own office, and Katy joined on as a full-time wealth manager working beside him. If you spoke to Andrew at this time, he'd tell you his primary focus in life was making more money. Although years away from learning to come ugly, even back then he knew this admission wasn't entirely true. Okay, Andrew didn't hold some deep, dark secret like an addiction problem, but his firm wasn't the only team he managed with relish—there was also the Newport Beach Seals.

Who—or what—were the Newport Beach Seals? A league of seventh- and eighth-grade boys who loved baseball just as much as Andrew—with one small catch. Their parents couldn't afford the pricey club programs in the area. Like any good market analyst, Andrew saw a hole in the market existed for boys who wanted to eventually play high school ball but inevitably fell behind. Why? They couldn't compete on the same level as middle schoolers who played travel baseball all summer.

The Seals quickly became Andrew's passion. He found more value in instructing boys and molding youths into young men than he ever did in his financial firm. For three joyful years he volunteered his time and scratched together resources for the boys to play. To their credit, and Andrew's, they performed at an unbelievable level. His Seals went 73-1 over three seasons against the best-funded teams in SoCal. Their prowess was all Andrew could talk about. (He once recounted a story to Power of 4 in which a colleague called to congratulate him on winning a major account. Momentarily confused, Andrew mistakenly thought he was talking about the tournament game his team won that past weekend.)

This brings you up to the time of the second Power of 4 meeting. Put simply, Andrew was a successful money manager—with the heart of a coach. He knew managing wealth wasn't his calling because he didn't gain satisfaction from it. Seeing players complete their first double-play combination meant much more to him than all his business wins *combined*. Knowing this, Andrew turned to Power of 4 for advice on the direction his life should take.

THE POWER OF 4 HELPS ANDREW CHART HIS COURSE

In just its second meeting, Power of 4 was taking on another big challenge. It was obvious Andrew had a talent and calling for coaching baseball, but he was trapped by his business accomplishments. The stats said it all. A renowned financial planner, Andrew pulled in upwards of $400,000 annually. As a college baseball coach, he only earned between $60,000 and $80,000.

What was he to do?

Andrew told the group he had a chance to get back into his previous profession but worried what the change would mean for his earning prospects and his marriage. As he laid out his dilemma, Bruce was the first to speak up. "You've made it clear you find coaching fulfilling. What do you think the best part of your interaction with players is?"

Andrew's eyes lit up at the chance to talk about his guys. "We have kids on the Seals that didn't think they'd be pitching past little league. Now they're getting scouted by the pros—as high schoolers. I've helped boys reach their potential while playing the game right. More importantly, I've showed them sportsmanship and how to be a man."

Steve, who knew a thing or two about this situation, added,

"Many of these kids don't have fathers in the home, yes? So, it's safe to say the impact you have on their life is more profound than helping a client earn a 5% higher return on their portfolio?"

"Absolutely. It's not even in the same ballpark." Mark nodded. Although he worked in a different area of the financial market, he was quite familiar with the business. "Andrew, you've built this firm by hard work, but if it's not your passion, I worry it'll inevitably sink."

Around the room, the other guys murmured similar fears for Andrew.

"How might a career change affect Katy?" Bruce asked. "Not as much as you might think. We really are in love and our relationship is strong—I know this because it's so unlike my last marriage. Moreover, she knows where my passion is, and she wants me to be a happy, fulfilled person. If I make the move to coaching, I know she'll support me."

Hearing this, Steve leaned in. "Glad to hear that. I have some connections in higher education. I know the Athletic Director at Vanguard University from his stint at Azusa Pacific University where I was Alumni Director. I can make that connection if you think it'll help."

The smile on Andrew's face said it all. This was just the thing he needed to pursue his calling, to take back his life. Based on that Power of 4 meeting and his own soul searching, Andrew created a plan. Over time, he handed the business over to his wife and partner while still retaining a smaller involvement level. He also took Steve up on his offer with Vanguard University, which was, by providence, rebuilding a struggling sports program.

Far more easily than he ever imagined, Andrew returned to God's design.

Before the year was out, Andrew was back coaching

baseball, molding young Christians into the leaders of tomorrow, and teaching Master's-level classes on the art of coaching to the next generation of coaches. Reflecting on his experience with Power of 4, he later told us, "I love going to work every day now. I can't believe it took me so long to figure things out, but I needed the viewpoints of men outside of my daily experience to see the light."

THE PRODIGAL SON RETURNED

Congratulations if you picked up on the obvious parallels between Andrew's career change and the Biblical story of the Prodigal Son. In Luke's Gospel, Jesus tells the story to explain why He associates with sinners. It tells the tale of two brothers, one of which blows town; like Andrew leaving his calling on the (figurative) baseball diamond. Receiving an early inheritance, he promptly sails away with it and blows it all on high living. He eventually returns home to his father and brother, the latter who remained perpetually faithful.

The father is overjoyed at the Prodigal Son's return and throws him a big party. This upsets the older brother, who can't understand why everyone is celebrating the jerk who wasted half of the family's wealth and brought great shame to them. According to scripture, the father's lesson to his faithful son is especially important: "And he said to him, 'Son, you have always been with me, and all that is mine is yours. But we had to celebrate and rejoice, because this brother of yours was dead and has begun to live, and was lost and has been found.' (Luke 15:31-32, NASB)"

Although not at all as wicked as the Prodigal Son, Andrew had become lost to materialism. Leaning on other men, he (re)found his true calling according to God's design, and the world is a better place for it. Andrew stopped worrying about dollars and put God first, a move made easier by coming ugly to Power of 4. In our next chapter, we will extend the metaphor of coming ugly to explore more disagreeable items: guile, duplicity, and inferiority.

CHAPTER 4

Come Ugly, Leave Clean

To open this chapter, let's take a break from the heavy lifting of confronting the challenges in our own lives and consider how most people interact with the Bible's wisdom. Ask a few people in your life this simple question: "Who said 'the truth will set you free?'" The range of answers you'll receive will be startling.

We commonly hear people attribute this famous phrase to leaders of the past. Whether it's JFK, RFK, or MLK, the leading lights of the 1960s often get credit for this saying—along with philosophers like Ralph Waldo Emerson. Of course, answers can vary with the age of the person you ask. A young liberal replied to one of the authors that former NFL quarterback and Black Lives Matter (BLM) activist Colin Kaepernick voiced these immortal words!

Of course, none of these individuals are responsible for the saying. These words were spoken by Jesus Christ, who rarely gets credit in modern society for His own teachings. In this case, Jesus was explaining the truth to the Jews in the Book of John, Chapter 8, after the Pharisees accused a woman of adultery. That story begins with another famous quote from our Lord, "He who is without sin among you, let him be the first to throw a stone at her. (John 8:7, NASB)" The latter part of this story is especially poignant to modern men wishing to improve themselves and walk the path God has laid out for us:

> So Jesus was saying to those Jews who had believed Him, "If you continue in My word, then you are truly My disciples; and you will know the truth, and the truth will set you free." They answered Him, "We are Abraham's descendants and have never been en-slaved to anyone; how is it that You say, 'You will be-come free'?"
>
> Jesus answered them, "Truly, truly I say to you, everyone who commits sin is a slave of sin. Now the slave does not remain in the house forever; the son does remain forever. So if the Son sets you free, you really will be free. I know that you are Abraham's de-scendants; yet you are seeking to kill Me, because My word has no place in you. I speak of the things which I have seen with My Father; therefore you also do the things which you heard from your father. (John 8:31-38, NASB)"

It's important to note the people Jesus spoke to were con-fused when He said, "The truth will set you free." They told Him they were never slaves, so they didn't understand how they could become free if they were *already* free. This is where we reach the part that Power of 4 considers critical. Jesus said, "Everyone who commits sin is a slave of sin." But, as we dis-cussed in chapter three, we are *all* fallen due to Adam's trans-gression. We are all sinners and, to varying degrees, slaves of sin. Power of 4 believes truth is critical, and our approach is encapsulated in the phrase "come ugly."

LIVE NOT BY LIES

As discussed in the last chapter, Power of 4 considers it vital that every brother comes to the group with vulnerability and transparency. The atmosphere is one of men speaking frankly about their problems. We show our true selves, "warts and all." Those of us that have spent time on a farm, like Steve growing up in rural Idaho, are most comfortable describing what we try to avoid: "putting lipstick on a pig." In other words, we wish to dispense with that thin veneer of success or glamour often effacing the truth.

Why? Most often, the truth concerns us men battling against our sense of inferiority. Feeling "less than" is a societal issue in America, as we will discuss at length later in this chapter. Some of us also experience imposter syndrome, in which we don't feel we deserve something or aren't good enough.

Other men feel intense pressure to be a movie star. But in SoCal, it's not good enough to be movie icon Harrison Ford. You must be his characters: Indiana Jones, Han Solo, and Jack Ryan, all rolled into one. In other words, it's natural to feel inferior when held up to an impossible manhood standard. When we men play the roles of success, when we pretend, we don't struggle with any form of inferiority, Power of 4 can do nothing for us.

PUTTING IN THE WORK

Naturally, you may wonder what Power of 4 can do when brothers *do* come ugly, dropping all pretense, embracing their vulnerability. Just to be clear, Power of 4 is no miracle cure for manhood. We don't *fix* people. Instead, we create an environment—or container—whereby men can do the work to fix *themselves,* hopefully discovering in the process a life-style most congruent with God's will.

When men unite in a group with full transparency and a commitment to humility, letting our vulnerability hang out, we benefit from myriad perspectives. What's more, we are primed to discover a higher degree of honesty with ourselves than we might dream possible. It's happened to every brother, and it can happen for you too. However, summoning the courage to be vulnerable and honest about one's life can still be a formidable challenge.

It certainly was for our brother Keith.

RIDING THE SURF, QUESTIONING LIFE

Not long ago, Keith was a successful executive in the surf industry. Readers from Boston, Chicago, and Seattle (not to mention, all points in between) may chuckle at that notion, but in SoCal—the surfing capital of the universe and home of the Beach Boys—surfing is big business. By nearly every measure, Keith's career was going gangbusters, and he wasn't chained to a desk all day either. He got plenty of time in the surf, traveled to exotic locales, and enjoyed partying with clients and colleagues on a regular basis.

But Keith's lifestyle had strayed from his faith. And this fact weighed on him as he continued through life. He began to see what separation from God had done to his family. The son of unhappily married parents (who were together for 68 years), tension, conflict, and belittling were the norm in his household. This experience had a devastating effect on future relationships; all his siblings divorced (two of them twice) from their spouses. He knew he didn't want his own marriage to suffer the same fate, but wondered if it was inevitable, as if they were all too broken to stay in a relationship, destined to pass it on to the next generation. Beyond this, Keith wished for his son to grow up to enjoy his own happy relationships.

In fact, it was through his son that Keith learned of a chance to change his life. And it all began through a different sport. Back then, Keith's boy Nicholas played lacrosse, coached by Mark. Keith witnessed firsthand the way the club molded young men, helping them make good choices guided by God. Keith recognized that he didn't have the luxury of a positive role model growing up, as his dad was physically around but not actually "fully present," and did not support him in his athletic endeavors. (Keith often felt left out and wanted his son to have a better team/sport experience.)

At last, Keith did what he later described as one of the hardest things in his life. After practice, pushing down his push anxiety, Keith approached Mark and said, "I need some help with my faith. Do you know what I can do?"

Looking back, both Mark and Steve recognize similar moments in their own faith journeys. Some of us had this conversation directly with God. Keith, on the other hand, had to do it the hard way, admitting to another man how lost he felt, how he needed direction. (No man asks for directions if they can help it, so Mark was struck by the vulnerability Keith willingly shared.)

It's not hard to guess what Mark suggested Keith do next. "You ought to come to church as my guest this weekend," he said. "It's step one to rekindling your relationship with God."

Inside, Keith knew that, despite everything that had happened in his life, God *was* always there. It was just that, if he was being honest, faith's importance had taken a distant position for most of his life.

Mark suggested Keith also attend a Power of 4 meeting. At that time, the group consisted of Steve, Mark, and two others.

Did this overture go well? Not so much. To begin with, Keith's wife and children thought the proposition odd. *"How is sitting around with a group of guys going to help anything?"* is likely one of the skeptical thoughts they had about the endeavor.

But Keith's detractors extended beyond his family—a Power of 4 brother was against him joining too. From the first time Mark mentioned Keith to the group, a brother named Bruce opposed the idea. Bruce doubted Keith's ability to be transparent about his problems. We don't really know *why* Bruce doubted Keith, but we suspect it was due to his material successes coming out of the surf industry.

Bruce harbored a distrust of Keith, and over time he made it known that he felt the addition may hurt him in the "real world." As Bruce explained it, he feared what might happen if Keith joined the group without coming ugly—without embracing the vulnerability and transparency that is the hallmark of everything we do. In Bruce's mind, if Bruce spoke transparently and Keith didn't, Bruce worried that his own personal issues would be exposed.

Was Bruce right to worry about this?

Years before, Bruce got involved leading a program for young entrepreneurs at a local charter school. He had participated in similar groups in his youth and felt it important to contribute to the next generation. When he heard the charter school didn't have a chamber for aspiring businessmen, Bruce met with the school's principal and stole a line from the baseball movie *Field of Dreams*, saying: "If [we] build it, [they] will come."

And indeed, young men and women came in droves. Bruce created a young entrepreneurs' program that evolved into an organization serving more than 100 area families. Keith had to remind Bruce that his daughter had participated in the club, loving every second of it. As it turned out, the two *were* connected in meaningful ways that Bruce didn't know about while he was doubting Keith's sincerity. In time, the shared connection melted the ice between Bruce and Keith, and this new brother was invited to attend his first Power of 4.

Little did he know just how much it would change his life.

KEITH COMES UGLY

When Keith began working with us, he embraced the core concept like it was tattooed on his forehead. "That's probably because I never felt free or secure enough to talk about my problems," he said. "Not even with myself."

And Keith's problems seemed endless, like a groundswell of good waves at dawn patrol.

Surfing, a central component of Keith's life, was one of the issues. His once legendary career was suffering. Though he was a gifted executive who put up strong numbers in his sector for years, it didn't matter. The surfing industry itself was going down the tubes—and we don't mean the huge waves immortalized in surf classics like *Point Break* and *The Endless Summer.* Overseas competition and brand consolidation had put the crunch on Keith, and at just the wrong time.

Beyond his professional challenges, Keith faced the looming threat of separation and divorce just like many of his family members had experienced. While plagued by mounting anxiety from what seemed like all sides, what overwhelmed him most was a growing sense of isolation in his core.

BREAKDOWN—BREAKTHROUGH

With the help of Power of 4, Keith did the hard work: unpacking his troubles. He also began reading the Bible and listening to it on CD while driving. He found the "Thru the

Bible" series by Dr. J. Vernon McGee to be particularly useful in understanding Christ's message. Through Bible study, attending church, and working with Power of 4, Keith uncovered things about himself once hidden behind an opaque screen.

For one thing, Keith began to understand and accept his mental issues. The anxiety he felt over so many aspects of his life weren't going away on their own and weren't likely to. Coming to grips with this meant changing his approach. He began exploring how he could manage his stresses on his own and with the help of others. As he did, he became a more transparent person, both within the group and, critically, with himself. Paying this boon forward, he found solace in helping others go through their pain, which, in turn, left him more equipped to deal with his own suffering.

Bottoming out in his career also turned out to be a blessing. No longer needing to play the role of the put-together professional he had so carefully crafted, he dropped the pretenses that he had kept up for years. As he began living a more authentic existence, the isolation he felt seemed to shrink daily. Taking this journey with Power of 4 also catalyzed a startling insight, one that has been a key component about our brotherhood ever since. Keith's life wasn't somehow magically made perfect by working hard with the group. Instead, it was put on a more positive *trajectory*, influencing his health, career, and family.

After several meetings with Power of 4 enabling such feelings, Keith felt comfortable to pose a question to the guys. "I'm curious," he began. "Why do you personally like coming to a Power of 4 meeting? I know why *I* come now, but what's the thing that adds a little pep to your step as you head out the door each time?" The men went around the table offering answers.

Steve began, "Well, I like these meetings because I come here with my equals. I can say what's on my mind and get perspectives that are dramatically different than my own. I, in turn, can share my views with others."

Mark chimed in next. "My Power of 4 meetings are the only time I can talk to men who aren't actively trying to stick a dagger in my back to get one rung higher on the corporate ladder." Though a dramatic statement, the others nodded in agreement.

Then Andrew, who never could avoid a baseball analogy, said, "This is my time where I don't have to send in signs to my team. I can get signs from my fellow coaches, and even if I shake them off, I know they're valuable."

Bruce went next. "The group helps me get closer to God, something I'm terrible at on my own. But what about you, Keith? What's your answer?" They all waited for their newest brother's insight.

"Talking to you guys is different than talking to my wife or a therapist. If these conversations could be bottled, they'd sell for a million bucks."

Everyone looked startled. We all knew somewhere in our hearts that a major part of Power of 4 is the difference in how we can talk between equal brothers as opposed to how we speak with our spouses or even a counselor; it's an extremely intimate relationship rooted in honesty. Still, this revelation hit Steve especially hard because he recognized the essential truth in what Keith said.

Later Steve reflected on this point. "I had been a therapist providing Christian support in various ways for decades by this point. Yet I'd never thought of it the way Keith laid it out at that meeting. A group of brothers committed to honesty and transparency *did* communicate quite differently from how I did with my patients, and it was certainly true that I communicated differently with Power of 4 than I ever did with my wife of many years. This concept has been our foundation ever since."

TALKING WITH YOUR WIFE VS. TALKING TO POWER OF 4

Some people would call it a "no brainer" that a group of men will speak differently with each other than they would with their wives. Those that see it this way might view marriage as a fundamentally *adversarial* relationship in which each spouse tries to keep the truth from their partner. On the other hand, any good marriage counselor will tell you that ideal matrimony is built upon *open* communication, a sharing of ideas, feelings, and opinions between a man and woman so the whole is greater than its two parts. Still, even in this latter, better situation, communication between a Power of 4 brother and his group will dramatically differ from speaking with one's wife.

To be sure, both relationships are important, and each deserve respect. In actuality, the respect for each brother's wife is the root cause of such differences in communication styles. Power of 4 is purposely designed to allow men to share things about ourselves that are of value to our marriage—but nonetheless could harm the emotional health of a man's partner. By our nature, we men typically withhold sharing things that might hurt our other half. Knowing this, Power of 4 creates a healthy outlet for those ideas to be expressed. Not to hide the truth, but rather, to unburden the man so he will practice and prepare to share with his wife. Especially so he can become a better husband.

Because Power of 4 brothers hail from different theological backgrounds, with a variety of practices and teachings about confession and forgiveness, it's important to point out that in our brotherhood, two passages of scripture especially guide us:

> James 5:16: "Therefore, confess your sins to one another, and pray for one another so that you may be healed. A prayer of a righteous person, when it is brought about, can accomplish much. (NASB)"

> Galatians 6:1-4: "Brothers and sisters, even if a person is caught in any wrongdoing, you who are spiritual are to restore such a person in a spirit of gentleness; each one looking to yourself, so that you are not tempted as well. Bear one another's burdens, and thereby fulfill the law of Christ. For if anyone thinks that he is something when he is nothing, he deceives himself. But each one must examine his own work, and then he will have reason for boasting, but to himself alone, and not to another. (NASB)"

When it comes to Power of 4, in a spirit of gentleness, our goal is to "fulfill the law of Christ" by confessing to our brothers and asking God's forgiveness with our brothers' prayerful support as part of daily living. Our experience has taught us that when one man is restored, that event impacts all his relationships, starting with his family.

As might be expected, over the years, Power of 4 has received its fair share of "confessions." We have listened as men have opened up about all kinds of issues, including:

* Pornography addiction

* Codependency and substance abuse

✳ The temptation of infidelity and the ever-present wan-
dering eye

All these topics easily possess the potential to shatter a
wife's ego, not to mention, hurt her feelings and undermine
trust. Yet, when handled sensitively and appropriately within
our brotherhood, these challenges can be worked on with
humility and faith via a trusting and a trustworthy group.
Also, Power of 4 discounts the idea that confessing sins—
whether to a priest or to a group of peers—is akin to throwing garbage over one's fence and expecting one's neighbor
to dispose of it. Instead, the garbage in this scenario should
be picked through to understand exactly where it came from,
then asking God to burn it away for you.

But let's be realistic.

There are many types of sin a man can experience or engage in that could cause their wives to reduce *them* to a pile of
ash, not their sins. It's therefore a fallacy that a man can share
absolutely anything with his wife. Imagine telling the woman
you wed that a gal in the office that's 20 years younger and
20 pounds lighter wears a thong every Friday that somehow
coordinates with your necktie—and makes sure you know it.

This information would needlessly freak her out, producing far more relationship problems than the girl at work
ever had the potential to cause on her own. Instead, we must
shepherd our wife just as the Lord shepherds us all.

How do we do that? Find the appropriate venue to confess. For men like us, this occurs in a group like Power of 4.
The Bible is full of lessons about confessing to one another
and, more importantly, forgiving each other. Although this
lesson is found throughout the Scriptures, we don't practice
it enough. It's like asking: "Which came first: the chicken or
the egg?"

Yet in this case, we *know* the egg came first. (The egg in this analogy is how we act ourselves.) Knowing this, we must learn to *practice* confession before we hear the confessions of others. We also need to practice forgiveness so we can learn how to bring forward a confession and forgive it. After all, just as in parenting, allowing someone else to confess their transgression is much more powerful than simply admonishing them for doing wrong.

Power of 4 also aids in a different but related way. By its nature, it provides each brother the perspective of three other men looking at you from all sides. *You* exist in the center of a group that doesn't care about your best camera angle or what you would prefer to leave in the shadows. Likewise, nothing is glossed over or obscured. There are no blind spots to hide in.

Instead, three different men provide you three perspectives that can sometimes differ radically. Since most people think monolithically, receiving these viewpoints on your life and its challenges is invaluable. You stand to gain clarity and opinions you might never have reached on your own. And, of course, these perspectives and advice tend to vary wildly from that which you might receive from having the same conversation with your wife.

THIS IS NOT TO GIVE YOU COVER

Importantly, Power of 4 brothers do not view the group as some excuse to not tell our wives important things. In most cases, informing the group does not mean you worked things out with your partner. However, it can impact how a later conversation may go—when you do finally talk to her. Think about it this way: Telling the group is like *practicing* with the guys. Consider it a rehearsal for an eventual conversation, but with the bonus of men providing their own perspectives, opinions, and experiences. Yes, sometimes, weighty issues *will* involve our wives, so preparing ahead of time, rather than just going in cold, can have a positive effect on her.

That said, although wives are not part of Power of 4, it's crucial that brothers make them feel involved, especially if we ever hope to gain their approval, much less show them its benefits. Also, we want our wives to feel like they're part of the process. (Which they are.) To assist with this mission, we maintain a couple simple rules: First, brothers don't share personal and/or confidential information about wives without receiving permission. (We may share vague or basic details, but nothing that would violate privacy.) Second, we make it clear that Power of 4 is all about becoming better men and better husbands. When wives understand these goals, it helps eliminate concerns.

Still, you can't blame wives for thinking the worst of a group of men. Inundated with the same pop culture propaganda we are, it's not hard to imagine how they may view the group: a gripe fest about the ladies divulged over cold beers. Without knowing what we are all about, it would be easy for females to dismiss Power of 4 as little more than a "Women Haters Club" or something out of a *The Three Stooges* short. But by involving wives, even in the application process, we impress upon them our outlook and our higher purpose. We tell them in no uncertain terms that Power of 4 is meant to improve each brother via the combined experiences and insights of like-minded men.

POSITIVE SUM GAME

When wives get involved in the process, they recognize the importance of men engaged in self-improvement, especially centered around faith. Also, the organizational dynamic of an effective Power of 4 group creates sanctification. *Daily* sanctification allows us the chance to do better in those relationships that matter most. And when devotion and purposeful thinking guide a man's life, he takes that blessing wherever he goes. Accordingly, our wives benefit, our children benefit, even our workplaces and communities benefit from the changes occurring within us. As Steve recalls, Mark's wife Margy "blamed" Steve for the changes she saw in Mark's life, but Steve wasn't the cause, *Mark* was. Steve was just another beneficiary of Mark's change for the better, along with Margy and the children—amongst many others.

For all these reasons and more, Power of 4 produces a special relationship only possible within a group of committed Christian men. As we are sure you're aware, too many pastors notoriously "fall in love" with female staff members because of deep spiritual conversations that cross over into the sensual. Power of 4, on the other hand, allows us men to foster brotherly love without an ounce of eros involved. This safe environment creates unique opportunities to share and learn without leading to risky behavior.

TALKING WITH YOUR THERAPIST VS. TALKING TO POWER OF 4

Steve jokingly points out the first big difference between a Power of 4 meeting and a therapist session is that you (or your insurance company) can pay a pretty penny for the privilege of speaking to the latter about your problems. Conversely, being in Power of 4 should cost nothing but your time. (And the occasional breakfast or coffee when brothers congregate.)

The other major difference is that those in therapy typically seek *understanding*, believing this will bring them peace and comfort. Let's explode that notion. It's time to ask yourself a hard question: Will understanding help?

That might sound like a funny thing to ask, but we're ready to "double down." *Is understanding overrated?* We think so. Just because you understand something doesn't guarantee you'll find peace or comfort in your understanding.

Power of 4 isn't hung up on understanding. Instead, we believe it's better to help a man realize that his fantasy of how life *should* unfold isn't always how the real world works. Only by separating our delusions from reality can we make progress as men in a relationship with God, our families, and our peers.

Also, therapy, by nature, is transactional. No one signs up for sessions with the idea of going to appointments for the rest of one's life. (Okay, unless you're a neurotic celebrity with cash to burn.) Power of 4 is instead about *relationships.* It's about crossing the finish line together. As such, we aren't problem solving. We are life solving. We aren't trying to fix other men. We are trying to walk with them. You can't shake your Power of 4 brothers unless you opt out or move away. And even when this happens, we'll still care about you.

And pray for you daily.

SO WHY DOES MODERN MAN FEEL SO INFERIOR?

Earlier we pointed out how practically every man we know has a sense of inferiority in some aspect. This is very much driven by being raised in a competitive culture where success and failure become a Catch-22. If we fail, we feel inferior. Yet if we succeed, we are scared to fail, leading to feeling inferior. Success doesn't tend to create a sense of encouragement in this paradigm. Rather, it just makes us fear failure more.

So many of us men worry about feeling shame. We live desperate existences trying to hide failures past, present, and future. Also, if we allow ourselves to play our roles, we worry someone will discover our true selves—that they will not like what they see.

This is a life centered on inferiority and not on one's authentic self.

But men are not only locked into a battle over feeling inferior, but also with feeling insecure. Insecurities are killers. They sap our energies, leading to self-doubt and loss of effectiveness in whatever we choose to do. Like one of Andrew's baseball players who might slip into a slump, wondering if they'd ever get another hit, insecurity gnaws away at all of us.

And, of course, insecurity naturally hits us hard in the workplace. At work, we wonder about being stabbed in the back, as Mark so eloquently put it. We worry someone might be promoted over us. It also affects our relationships. Here we wonder if our spouse is actually glad that she married us in the first place. It hits us with our families, too. Here we wonder if we can ever be a better parent. Or even a good parent at all.

But insecurities and feelings of inferiority are just the beginning. They get compounded by our conscious actions. What types of negative choices do you continually make in your life? Power of 4 has heard many over the years and tried to help each man overcome them. Here is a brief list of some bad behaviors we've discussed within our group:

* Abuse (in various forms)

* Addiction

* Improper alcohol and drug use

* Foul language usage

* Poor parenting choices

* Lying/cheating at work and at home

If you regularly participate in these bad behaviors (or any other) and cannot confess them, they hold real power over you. Remember, in John 8:34, Jesus taught "Truly, truly I say to you, everyone who commits sin is a slave of sin. (NASB)" We tend to think of addicts or people trapped by negative behaviors as being the lowliest in society, but it can and does happen at each level of success, because inferiority exists at every level. Consider the successful career man pulling in more than $200,000 annually. By any measure, even that of The OC, this guy seems to be doing well in his profession.

But he isn't necessarily free from vices. In fact, he's likely trying to cover the pain of inferiority just like anyone else. And now he has the income to become a *functional* addict, which is a trap many of us fall into. The world sees the veneer of professional success, while in reality, this man is likely surreptitiously watching porn in high-risk situations that would get him fired whilst drinking enough to still be hungover in an afternoon client presentation.

How did modern man get here—even our winning guy with his admirable salary? The short answer is that recent generations face negative forces even our parents didn't face. These don't only impact us directly, but also indirectly by poisoning the minds of the women and children surrounding us. The first of these negative forces is the media. Modern TV and movies offer a steady drumbeat of negative male stereotypes. Even those shows that seem to establish masculine role models, like *Mad Men,* teach us to lie, steal, and commit adultery. The rare outliers seem to offer examples few of us will ever measure up to.

Is it any wonder this situation is in part responsible for the newest buzzword? As noted, the damaging concept of "toxic masculinity" is a vast attempt to destroy everything about what it means to be a man. Its widespread acceptance has led to a breakdown of the family and even questioning of gender roles. But we wouldn't have gotten here without an active media working overtime to destroy the head of the household. (If you want our advice, stop worrying about people's pronouns—call them by their first names.)

The second negative factor is the wave of disdain for men in society. Specifically white, Christian men seem to be enemy number one for academia, media, and the political left, not to mention those running Silicon Valley. We are left wondering if we should fight against this trend and stubbornly stand up for our fellow brothers—knowing that many won't stand up even for themselves. Instead, too many men go along with nonsense like "mansplaining" and the "evils of patriarchy."

Clearly, older generations didn't have the added stressors of a corrupt media and a prevailing cultural disdain for manhood—on top of pressures men already faced. Unfortunately, we must acknowledge there is no roadmap through this mess. Still, we have a better chance of navigating it together instead of on our own. As the Three Musketeers said in Alexandre Dumas' famous novel, "All for one, one for all."

In our next chapter, we'll talk about what happens when a brother doesn't live up to the promise we just set out; when he instead rejects the entire essence of what it means to "come ugly."

CHAPTER 5

What If One of Us Fails to Live Up to Power of 4?

Betrayal.

It's one of those words in the English language that can send a chill down your spine. When someone deceives their friends or turns traitor against their country or faith, the story is always juicy. When you read that single word to start this chapter, what did your mind immediately turn to?

Because we live in the modern world with much of our culture shaped by movies and TV, you might have thought of the silver screen, where some of the best films ever made featured betrayals. One classic example comes from *The Godfather Part II*, in which mob boss Michael Corleone is betrayed by his weak brother Fredo. Michael embraces Fredo, delivering the immortal line: "I know it was you, Fredo. You broke my heart. You broke my heart."

The name Fredo has become synonymous with "traitor" based on *The Godfather*, but it's far from the only infamous fictional betrayal. Younger men may recall how Han Solo's old gambling pal Lando Calrissian sold him out in *The Empire Strikes Back*. Luckily for the rebel alliance, Lando turns back into a hero before the *Star Wars* trilogy concludes, rising to the occasion by leading an assault on the Death Star.

Of course, betrayal isn't limited to Tinseltown fare. History books are chock-full of betrayals, too. The times, they may change, but human nature does not. And in fact, the great deceptions of record were typically based in this sin.

Take the traitor Benedict Arnold. Once a strong field general and loyal to the *American* rebel cause, he changed sides when he didn't receive enough credit to please his ego. "Through his wife, Arnold contacted Major John André, Adjutant General and intelligence chief to British Commanding General Sir Henry Clinton, proposing to turn over West Point in exchange for a large payment," according to intelligence.gov. "He offered an additional lure, the potential capture of George Washington during a planned visit. The British readily agreed." Likewise, infamous spies like Aldrich Ames and Robert Hanssen peddled our secrets to the former Soviet Union for cold, hard cash.

And yet, sometimes, the reason betrayals happen aren't so clear. The motivation behind one of the greatest betrayals of all time—when Brutus joined a group of Roman senators in assassinating his uncle and adoptive father Julius Caesar—is debated to this day. Regardless of rationale, all these real-life betrayals impacted the world, yet pale in comparison to the ultimate betrayal—the treachery committed against our Lord.

JUDAS BETRAYED JESUS FOR A LOUSY PAYDAY

Jesus made many enemies through his teachings, among them what Matthew 26:3 terms "the chief priests and the elders of the people. (NASB)" These wicked men ultimately gathered at the home of high priest Caiaphas to devise a plot to arrest and kill our Savior. The only problem? In movie parlance, they needed an "inside man."

They found this in the form of Judas Iscariot. The father

of the Reformation, Martin Luther, once said: "Each betrayal begins with trust." This was certainly true in Judas' case. He was one of the disciples, a trusted figure. Nevertheless, he sold Jesus out to the authorities for 30 pieces of silver, as documented in the Book of Matthew, Chapter 26:

> Then one of the twelve, named Judas Iscariot, went to the chief priests and said, "What are you willing to give me to betray Him to you?" And they set out for him thirty pieces of silver. And from then on he looked for a good opportunity to betray Jesus. (Matthew 26:14-16, NASB)

Jesus even predicted Judas' betrayal at the Last Supper, stating in Matthew 26:23: "He who dipped his hand with Me in the bowl is the one who will betray Me. (NASB)" Treacherous Judas, who had already taken the bribe and planned to betray Jesus, answered him with a denial in Matthew 26:25: "Surely it is not I, Rabbi? (NASB)"

Despite the denial, the scene was set for Judas' ultimate betrayal of Jesus at the Mount of Olives.

> And while He was still speaking, behold, Judas, one of the twelve, came accompanied by a large crowd with swords and clubs, who came from the chief priests and elders of the people. Now he who was betraying Him gave them a sign previously, saying, "Whomever I kiss, He is the one; arrest Him." And immediately Judas went up to Jesus and said, "Greetings, Rabbi!" and kissed Him. But Jesus said to him, "Friend, do what you have come for." Then they came and laid hands on Jesus and arrested Him. (Matthew 26:47-50, NASB)

The rest of the story is the topic of our Easter holiday. Jesus knew He would be betrayed, but still He accepted the treachery and His death on the cross to redeem us from our sins. What we don't think so much about is how Judas turned traitor so cheaply.

That topic has been studied by economist, and contributor to *The Christian Post*, Jerry Bowyer. Bowyer compares the bribe Judas received, 30 pieces of silver, with the cost of the expensive fragrance gifted to Jesus in Matthew 26:6-13. Such favor seems to have been a primary motivator for Judas' eventual betrayal. As Bowyer writes:

> Mary uses an expensive jar of nard, a spice imported from the East, which we are told is worth 300 denarii, amounting to almost a year's wages. Judas raises an objection to the expense, and the Bible alludes to the fact that he will later hand Jesus over, which we know he did for money.
>
> If Judas' 30 pieces of silver refer to the same coinage Judas claims the gift of perfume is worth (which is quite plausible given that denarii were silver), then Judas betrayed Jesus for a mere tenth (a tithe) of the amount Mary gave to Jesus to honor Him. Judas' betrayal of Jesus came cheap.
>
> On the other hand, it is possible that the temple elite paid him in Tyrian shekels, which were worth about 120 denarii, but even that is still less than half of Mary's offering. Her sacrifice to the glory of Christ is more than Judas' reward for betraying Him.

For many Christians, just trying to imagine betraying Jesus during His life on earth is shocking—especially from one of the disciples, who knew Him better than anyone. Although no duplicity in this mortal realm will ever match this offense, sadly, betrayals—both petty and large—happen daily. And Martin Luther was right. Betrayal can't happen unless trust occurs first. This means that groups like Power of 4, built upon goodwill between like-minded men, are still likely to face betrayal at some point.

Our group certainly has on more than one occasion. This chapter is dedicated to one such story and what we learned from it. As it so happens, what we went through wasn't nearly as dramatic as that found in the movies or the history books, thank God. In fact, it's fair to say Bruce only betrayed our group in a secondary way—the true betrayal was to himself.

You see, Bruce was a Power of 4 brother for years, but the whole time he was living a lie. He refused to come ugly, and this was his downfall. Not to spoil the ending, as the kids say, but like Lando Calrissian in *Star Wars*, Bruce ultimately came back to God's side. The takeaway from his story is not the juicy details of his sins and the problems they caused, but how Power of 4 dealt with them and enabled him to make amends.

HOW BRUCE JOINED OUR GROUP

Bruce had been an athlete his entire life. He played baseball and football on the varsity teams in high school, then just football in college. Although he didn't play for a major college football powerhouse, it was nonetheless a team that excelled in its conference. He wasn't a star player, but he was a first stringer, and this experience set his mind on a career track related to sports.

For the first few years of college, Bruce dreamed of joining the NFL as a pro. A realistic discussion about his chances with the coaching staff deflated that dream quickly. As his coach explained, he was a solid college player, not an elite one destined for the big time. This led to several months of Bruce feeling lost. Sports were his life. What could he do if he wasn't going to be on the gridiron? Over Christmas break during his junior year, he had an epiphany. Like Jim, he could combine his love of sports with his natural business skills to remain *close* to the field, even if he would no longer be in competition after his final season. Also, like Keith, Bruce's plan was to break into the sporting industry.

Bruce's mentors were on board with his plan. As a football player, he had already gained deep insights into how college teams and equipment suppliers interacted. He had noticed that most had trouble balancing cost and quality. Either they entered with the cheapest prices selling junk, or they came in with an insanely high quote for the finest gear. From Bruce's perspective, he could do it better by finding a happy medium that would best suit most universities, high schools, and club teams.

Bruce's approach worked well for decades. He rose up the executive ranks to be a senior leader at one of the largest sporting goods companies in the nation, and times were good. But as we moved into the 2000s, sporting goods changed. Superior American-made products were replaced by low-quality fare made in China, even from major companies. At the same time, even small schools were demanding free equipment, since companies like Nike and Reebok threw around money like it grew on trees.

Around this time, Bruce started the young entrepreneurs club we mentioned in chapter four. As the club grew, Bruce had to make hard choices. The first involved how devoted to the club he wished to be. Already, he was struggling to keep his corporate job while managing the club. And as his duties to the program increased, his business suffered. Second, Bruce had to make choices about his own life. Yes, the club was thriving, but he was not.

Seeing Bruce in a spiritual crisis, a friend recommended Bruce talk to Steve, who had mentored the friend successfully through a variety of issues. Steve immediately recognized that Bruce didn't need a mentor, he needed a group of equals, so he suggested Bruce consider Power of 4.

Recommending another man join the group isn't something done lightly. This isn't a multi-level marketing outfit where bringing in fresh blood is required. Still, as your group establishes a successful track record, you will likely find men that can benefit from it. Since our numbers naturally shift over time, it isn't uncommon to have a few prospects in mind before an opportunity exists for someone to join.

Steve sensed ways the group could improve Bruce's situation, should he get involved. For instance, Bruce frequently told Steve about his lack of role models growing up. The few men he eventually looked up to came in the form of corporate executives, but that's a very different environment compared to the world outside of big business.

Next, Bruce told Steve his family had a history of alcoholism, gambling, and other illicit behaviors that he would only hint at. From Steve's position, Bruce was a guy who was doing good in the world, yet was spiritually adrift, suffering emotionally and mentally. After discussing it with the other brothers, Steve invited Bruce to join Power of 4, inadvertently setting in motion what would become a difficult phase in our organization's history.

Before delving into what happened, let it be clear we

welcomed Bruce with open arms, having no clue we were journeying down a path that would force us to answer disturbing questions, including:

* What do you do when a man won't tell the truth about how he lives his life?

* What do you do when a man won't disclose addictions?

* What do you do when a man flat-out lies about things, like his finances?

For his part, Bruce may have thought he was "coming ugly" to meetings when he was fighting an obvious hangover or even a lingering buzz, but, in fact, he never really opened up to the group and came clean—about many things.

WARNING SIGNS OF A GROUP WITH A PROBLEM

As you know by now, Power of 4 was founded on the idea that men with good intentions can meet to help each other be better men and Christians. Well intentioned or not, no instruction manual existed for us to follow in the beginning. In fact, you're reading our attempt to fix that right now! While so many aspects of our organization "just worked" from that first meeting, what we weren't equipped to do was immediately spot signs of a troublesome brother. (Just because a man has challenges doesn't mean *he's* a problem. He only becomes one when he violates our honesty oath.)

Also, what follows is not intended to be a gripe session. Rather, it's to demonstrate how deceit is perhaps even more damaging to a high-trust group, like Power of 4, than it is in general life. Back when Bruce first joined, we knew he wasn't a perfect person. Newsflash: *None* of us are flawless. By our nature, we are fallen creatures. Our purpose is not to seek perfection. It's about doing better, and Bruce seemed intent on that.

As we got to know Bruce, we recognized a family history of codependent behaviors that left Bruce without the support network men require. What we didn't know: The full extent of Bruce's problems, and his unwillingness to own his truth. It would be nearly a decade before these things became obvious.

The first indicator of a deeper issue concerned how Bruce approached meetings. Almost from the outset, Bruce tended to monopolize sessions. That is, *if* he spoke at all. You see, he acted like a light switch. Either he was "on," sucking up the entire time to discuss his problems, or he was "off," hardly adding to the discussion, no matter the topic.

Bruce's behavior caused obvious challenges. Our brothers began to privately complain to each other. One man even remarked to Steve, "When did 'Power of 4' become 'Power of Listening to Bruce?'"

What was occurring clearly represented a misunderstanding of the group's dynamics. Bruce didn't treat Power of 4 as men uniting to help each other. He seemed to consider meetings to be an Alcoholics-Anonymous-style endeavor. Or as Steve puts it, "Groups like AA have no crosstalk between members and recognize a complete lack of control over addiction. That program works well for its members, but it isn't what Power of 4 does. Our group—similar in some respects to therapy—concentrates on finding those life areas we can control and seeks to help men improve in them."

At the time, Steve and the others also observed how Bruce would place blame for his problems on addiction. Doing so freed him to abdicate his responsibility. "He would refuse to work on either that particular problem or the many others that would spring up around it," Mark explains.

This wasn't the only sign of addict behavior that is obvious in retrospect. It's clear now that Power of 4 never needed an attendance system. Our culture has always been about *wanting* to be there—but this didn't hold true with Bruce. He would randomly disappear for two or three meetings in a row, then reappear as if nothing had happened.

Before long, Power of 4 devolved into two groups: the unit with Bruce there, and the one without. "Thankfully, meetings went on normally without him in time because we were strong enough to be flexible to fit the situation," adds Mark. "But it wore on us. In all honesty, there was sometimes a collective sigh of relief when Bruce was absent—along with his sordid tales in which he was somehow always the victim."

You see, *how* Bruce shared his challenges was perhaps the single greatest problem he brought to the table. His fellow brothers were transparent and honest about their situations; however ugly they might have been. Bruce, on the other hand, would recount highly editorialized versions of events.

As Steve explains, "Our brother would lay out details in such a way that made it painfully obvious to all he wasn't telling us even half of the actual story. Worse, he would hold the group accountable if he didn't like our input."

Here's an example. One time, Bruce spent nearly an entire meeting ranting about a negative interaction with a coach at the charter school where his entrepreneurs' club met. Still, somehow, he skirted around what touched off the problem. We later learned the teacher had caught him placing sports bets using an office phone—a reasonable thing to oppose in a charter school.

As it turns out, Bruce's editorializing went beyond the facts of a problem to what he chose to share in the first place.

His obvious distrust of his fellow brothers led them to hold back out of concern they were being too trusting. But there were even more problems. "Bruce was a big believer in what we call *trickle-truth*," Keith explains. "Instead of coming ugly, he'd ignore the elephant in the room to talk about a smaller issue. We'd hear about a tiff with a parent in the business club instead of getting to the bottom of a topic."

To Keith's point, even after broaching a difficult subject, it would be shared with us little by little, like Bruce was trying to boil frogs instead of coming together with his peers. This was certainly true with Bruce's gambling, which eventually reached the crisis point of extreme addiction.

The problems didn't stop there, unfortunately. The headaches Bruce caused us all weren't limited to meetings. Unlike other brothers who shared their challenges in the *group* setting, Bruce developed the habit of unloading on a one-on-one basis. He would make another man swear not to tell the others for fear of losing his reputation.

This happened with Steve. Several times, Bruce would invite him to lunch in a friendly way, only to spring a major issue on him. It also occurred with Keith. Purposefully or not, Bruce placed the other man in a real bind each time he did this. *Should they respect Bruce's right to tell the group on his terms, or should they spill their guts at the next meeting?* Brothers were left to wonder.

Such communications simply aren't in the spirit of Power of 4. Sharing an issue outside of the group isn't a bad thing. But it shouldn't become common, and it certainly shouldn't occur in secret. This may sound like an awful time for us, but ironically, Bruce's poor behavior showed us our group was *working*. For all his duplicity, Bruce was witnessing men coming ugly, taking ownership of their problems, and collaborating to improve as men and become closer to God.

Despite all of this, Power of 4 just wasn't enough for Bruce. He was headed for a severe crisis—with our help or without it.

HOW BRUCE HIT ROCK BOTTOM

One day, Bruce surprised us all in our breakfast meeting when he rushed into the room, out of breath. We stared in wonder at this disheveled man with the hair sticking up and bloodshot eyes.

"Debbie caught me last night," he said, chugging a glass of water.

"What does that mean?" Steve asked.

Bruce proceeded to hand over his phone. On it were a series of pornographic images his wife must have screenshot off a video.

"It's all over," he told us.

"Debbie's divorcing you?" Andrew asked.

"No, but she did force me to sign up for a sexual addiction program at my church."

After this admission, Bruce came ugly for the first time. It turned out, this moment was really the tip of the iceberg. Bruce was also suffering from relationships/intimacy issues with Debbie. It didn't help that he was treating his own anxiety and depression with a variety of substances.

Alarmed to say the least, Mark counseled him that the first thing he needed to do was also bring this to the group so we could provide him guidance beyond what one man could provide on his own. Unfortunately, Bruce didn't *completely* take this advice. Although Bruce swore up and down that he was finally ready to come ugly, he never got to the level of truth that Power of 4 could turn into actionable advice.

He stubbornly maintained that he wasn't an addict.

Despite repeated behaviors that are clear addiction signs, he held on to the fact that he didn't have a real problem. He didn't consider his use of substances to be a significant factor in what led to his recent troubles. Still, the confrontation with Debbie over his porn watching, in Bruce's own words, was a "slip-up that shouldn't have happened."

From here, Bruce's life went downhill faster. Even at this point, Power of 4 didn't abandon Bruce. Although he often skipped meetings and church, we stayed devoted to him without judgment. We'd hear him out when he called us at odd or early hours. We'd listen to him cry to us sometimes because he was so lost at that point. We never deserted him, and eventually it paid off.

In his darkest hour, Bruce was led back to Jesus Christ. Power of 4 can't take credit, though. We can say that it was God's grace through faith in Jesus Christ that convinced Bruce to turn to the Lord for help. He later told us, in his first experience coming ugly for real, that he was watching a beautiful sunset when he was inspired to fall to his knees and pray like he had never prayed before. He prayed for the strength to walk away from all his vices and demons. As Bruce explained, he cried like he hadn't since he was six years old, begging God for another chance.

Bruce's "second act" involved many forms. He entered an inpatient program to get clean under medical supervision. He also began attending marriage counseling and swore off pornography forever. After several months of intense dedication, he returned to Power of 4 to update us on his recovery.

From the start of the meeting, it was clear Bruce felt regret about his behavior and the problems it had caused all of us. But we didn't browbeat him or blame him. We forgave him. We celebrated his rekindled relationship with God, his sobriety, and his willingness to return to us with the whole truth.

POWER OF 4

POWER OF 4 NEEDED
THE POWER OF BALANCE

Without really knowing it at the time, the way we handled
Bruce's problems was to constantly balance truth and love.
We never bludgeoned Bruce over the head with demands,
instead tempering our approach with kindness and patience.
Author John MacArthur writes about this critical give-and-
take in his excellent book *40 Lives in 40 Days*.

In a section about the Apostle John, MacArthur writes:

> John was always committed to truth, and there's cer-
> tainly nothing wrong with that, but it is not enough.
> Zeal for the truth must be balanced by love for peo-
> ple. Truth without love has no decency; it's just bru-
> tality. On the other hand, love without the truth has
> no character; it's just hypocrisy.
>
> Many people are just as imbalanced as John was,
> only in the other direction. They place to much em-
> phasis on the love side of the fulcrum. They talk a lot
> about love and tolerance, but they utterly lack any
> concern for the truth. On the other hand, there are
> many who have all their theological ducks in a row
> and know their doctrine but are unloving and self-ex-
> alting. Their lack of love cripples the power of truth
> they profess to revere.
>
> The truly godly person must cultivate both virtues
> in equal proportions. Know the truth and uphold it
> in love.

Our attempts to help Bruce face the truth and find God
were also solidly rooted in the scriptures which Power of 4
takes inspiration from. The Book of Mark, Chapter 2, tells a

story (also found in the Book of Matthew, Chapter 9) about Jesus preaching at Capernaum.

A group of four men approach the gathered crowd with a special task:

> And some people came, bringing to Him a man who was paralyzed, carried by four men. And when they were unable to get to Him because of the crowd, they removed the roof above Him; and after digging an opening, they let down the pallet on which the paralyzed man was lying. And Jesus, seeing their faith, said to the paralyzed man, "Son, your sins are forgiven. (Mark 2:3-5, NASB)"

The four men carrying the paralyzed man to Jesus provided ongoing inspiration to Power of 4 throughout this difficult time. We so hoped that Bruce, paralyzed by sin, would be forgiven, just as the man in the Bible. By the grace of God, he very much was, and we pray we are forgiven our sins as well.

MANY MEN ARE ALLERGIC TO TRANSPARENCY

Often men struggle with being fully honest in a group setting like Power of 4. This is because there is a wider *societal* fear concerning transparency. Yet we know coming ugly creates depths of intimacy not possible when men only show their peers what they want seen. Of course, men fearing intimacy is nothing new in our culture, it's classic "avoider behavior."

In fact, this fear has been scientifically documented. As Dr. Seth Meyers asked in a *Psychology Today* article ("Fear of Intimacy in Men: Cause, Relationship Problems, Tips"), "Do men fear relationships more than women? The truth is that it's hard to tell. Measuring fear of intimacy among men and women in a research sense is tricky, but one study (Thelen et al., 2000) attempted it and found that men scored higher on a Fear-of-Intimacy Scale. To women who have known men terrified of relationships, this research will come as no surprise."

Men trapped by a fear of intimacy avoid problems by staying busy. They also compartmentalize. The thinking goes, everything, but especially negative things, are meant to remain in their perfect little box with no spillover. But then along comes something like an addiction or transgression. When either shows up, they can burst those boxes apart, causing all kinds of mayhem. Ultimately, this life approach doesn't work because there's one important characteristic to each of us that we can't fit in a single assigned box: our character.

In fact, it goes into *every* box we create.

A CRISIS OF TRUST

Most every man wants to be trusted, and to trust the men around them. This is especially true in a group like Power of 4, which is a high-trust organization. But this is easier said than done in a world filled with scams, greed, scandals, and the suspicion *anyone* could be out to get you—to betray you. Of course, lack of trust is a much larger societal problem than anything confined to Power of 4. According to the Edelman Trust Barometer, which runs surveys in 28 countries to gauge how average people trust governments, the media, and even charities, faith in our institutions has plummeted in recent years.

Okay. Most Americans feel it is *healthy* to distrust the bureaucrats and politicians living high on the hog with our tax dollars—that's baked into our individualistic culture. Even so, it's still yet another clear sign that so much of the goodwill that once held our civilization together is eroding—rapidly.

From not only our experiences with Bruce, but also many other examples of behavior influenced by substance abuse and other vices, there are four kinds of deception to be on the lookout for, especially for men committed to establishing their own groups. Some forms of duplicity may appear more innocent than others, but all can lead to greater problems, whether they exist amongst your brotherhood or in other environments, like the workplace.

Intentional Deception

Perhaps the most wicked type of treachery, this involves outright lying. When a hungover man asks you to believe he hasn't been drinking—instead of trusting your lying eyes—he's intentionally deceiving you.

Deception by Omission

Often, it's not what a man says, but what he *doesn't* say. Sometimes brothers tell us the least important details while at the same time leaving out the important stuff.

Unintentional Omission

Typically done innocently and often by accident, key details may be left out of a group discussion because a brother believes them to be unimportant or not relevant. Steve's infamous milkshake story, found later in this book, offers a prime example.

Multilayered Deception

Sometimes men combine various forms of duplicity to present a picture of themselves that isn't accurate. This is particularly common with new brothers who don't know to what degree they can trust the group. Consider the tendency of people to post pictures to social media that show an idealized version of their life instead of coming ugly.

WHAT WE LEARNED FROM BRUCE

Bruce's time with our group ended positively. We remain in touch with him, as with other brothers who have left. Even better, he's sworn off gambling and his other vices. We're proud of him and we're happy for Power of 4, too. We learned that what we do *works*. We didn't slam the door shut when we knew Bruce wasn't being honest, because we knew the Lord wouldn't slam the door on him either.

Instead, we tried to support him by balancing truth and love.

Through this challenge, we learned the importance of maintaining positive group dynamics. One brother's difficulties cannot be allowed to create problems for everyone else. That is another form of balance best learned through experience. The final lesson that Bruce's story makes clear is that Power of 4 isn't here to magically fix any man. Instead, we create an environment (or the aforementioned "container") for positive interaction between equals, offering advice from diverse viewpoints to help brothers work on themselves. In Bruce's case, when he fixed his relationship with God, everything else fell into place.

CHAPTER 6

What's the Biggest Thing Missing in Life Today?

Rodney (Rod) was a brother in our group for only a few years, but he didn't leave under negative circumstances. Instead, he relocated to Texas for a major opportunity he couldn't pass up. (This is a natural part of Power of 4. Not everyone is a long-term brother, but they become a brother in Christ forever.)

We'll never forget the time he showed up to a meeting pale, looking like he just saw a ghost. It's a tale we still discuss with him whenever we catch up. But first, more on Rodney's history.

He moved from the San Francisco Bay area (The Bay) to The OC for work reasons in 2012. Through mutual friends, he was introduced to Steve, who spent his high school years in what would later become Silicon Valley. The two hit it off, and by 2013, Rod had officially joined Power of 4. He was what we'd consider a typical brother—a man interested in being closer to God and making better decisions concerning his career and family life.

But, as we said, one day that first year he showed up to our meeting looking as white as a sheet. It was obvious something had surprised him—and not in a good way. Mark picked up on his attitude first. "Rodney, you look spooked—literally. What happened?"

"Yeah, something really strange. It goes back ten years though, so I'll have to give you some context. Anyone mind if I go first today?"

Rodney made his request out of politeness. As soon as the rest of us caught on to what Mark noticed first, there was no way someone else would take center stage. Looking back, we joke that at least half the group would have staged a mutiny if anyone objected to Rodney telling his tale.

PARTNERSHIP, SILICON VALLEY STYLE

Rodney built a career as a smart, capable software engineer working for various *old-guard* tech companies—the kind lacking a "dot-com" in their name. He made an excellent living at the time. Better yet, property values were exploding in the early 2000s as America enjoyed the Internet revolution, seemingly unaware the dot-com "bubble" would soon burst.

Rodney and several coworkers sensed that the fledgling web had the potential to transform the business world, but it wasn't quite there yet. (Remember, back in 2003 the internet still seemed like a novelty. Few thought we'd be using it for everything from teleconferencing to filing our taxes.) What Rod and his two coworkers, Neil and Chris, observed was that many upstart web companies were typically run by 20-somethings focused on end-user consumers. These savvy entrepreneurs, for all their skills, didn't know yet how to work with larger, traditional hardware and software entities.

Accordingly, the three insiders recognized a unique opportunity. People like them—those who understood the power of the internet and had experience with the big players—could act as "translators." They could create tools and business practices to help startups better deal with veteran companies that had been around longer than the entrepreneurs (and sometimes their parents) had even been alive.

Forming a partnership on a handshake, they set out their shingle as a consultancy firm. Rodney and Chris, affectionately called the "code monkeys," spent their time producing effective software for startups to collaborate with the likes of Netscape. Meanwhile, charismatic Neil was the sales guy pressing the flesh, making the deals. Note: All this occurred on the *side* for Rodney. He (wisely) kept his day job because his family needed stable income.

At first, things went great. All three men provided an exceptional service to the new Silicon Valley economy. Soon, word got around that they were the new go-to guys. Each was making serious money by then. Pretty soon they had to bring on part-time help as their business expanded.

Even so, things remained informal between the trio. Eventually, Neil made the company official and shoved some documents before Rodney to sign. He did so without thinking, because, as Rodney explains, "It was a partnership amongst friends. What could go wrong?" Unfortunately, a lot can—especially when money is concerned.

October 8, 2003, was a typical fall day in The Bay. After leaving his day job, Rodney planned to drop in at the consultancy to tweak code for their latest client. When he got to the door, Neil and Chris were waiting. A grim look on his face, Neil said, "Rodney, we need to speak to you right now."

Alarmed, Rodney followed him into their conference space. Without warning, Neil dropped the bomb. "Rodney, you haven't been holding up your end of things around here. We've voted you out of the partnership. You'll get a cash payment for your third, but we don't want you here anymore. Get your stuff and head out."

Rod was floored. He had invested his free time *and* sweat into making their enterprise a success. Now his "supposed" friends and partners were pulling the rug out from under him. The only reply he could manage was a simple one: "Y-you can't do this to me."

Neil smiled. "Oh yeah, we can. It's right there in the deal agreement you signed last month. You *did* read it, didn't you?"

Rodney noticed Chris wouldn't meet his eyes. "Why would I? I thought we were buddies."

Although some more back and forth went on, Rodney left defeated. Neil was right. The agreement he signed allowed for a partner to be voted out. He received a cash payout of $100,000 for his third and went on his way.

It wasn't long before he learned *why* all this occurred. It had a lot to do with the subject of our last chapter: betrayal. It turned out, several months after he was booted from his own startup, an established software company absorbed the consultancy for a cool $3 million. His "buddies" had cut him over $900,000.

Shocked, Rodney considered legal action, then gave up on the idea and moved on with his life. If anything, he felt comfort knowing there was a real reason, treacherous as it was, to dissolve the partnership—instead of his partners' claims that he did bad work. Obviously, he avoided contact with the two men who betrayed him, which wasn't hard considering he didn't run into them in the office after their big payday.

Fast forward a decade to 2013. Rodney was content, working as an IT leader for a major entertainment company, attending church with his family, and enjoying regular Power of 4 meetings. On the Saturday before our usual one, there was a knock at his door.

Rodney opened it without thinking twice. On the doorstep was his old buddy Chris. Clearly, he had aged hard over the last decade. This time, he met Rodney's eyes. "Can I talk to you for a few minutes?" he asked.

Chris came to Rodney to repair the damage done a decade ago. He started by explaining why he was there. Chris had developed a substance abuse problem even before the partnership started, and as part of his 12-step recovery program, he had to right past wrongs. He explained his side this way: "It was Neil's plan. He got in my head. He convinced me you weren't helping enough, and you were gonna get rich off our hard work. I foolishly listened."

Chris admitted he did a horrible thing and asked Rodney for forgiveness. He then beat a hasty retreat knowing he had ambushed his old friend showing up unannounced. Still, he asked Rodney to get in touch if he could find it in his heart to absolve his former partner.

This brings us up to the day Rodney met with us. We were all listening with rapt attention, hanging on his every word. When he finished, Keith chimed in: "That's a helluva story, Rod. How do you feel about it now?"

* * *

Before we tell you what happened next, we must discuss something vital. Something that's unfortunately disappearing at incredible speed in America: forgiveness. Forgiveness is something we all crave at times, but many of us hate giving. It also isn't easy to develop the ability to forgive. If young people especially could mine forgiveness as they do Bitcoin, they might not get rich, but their lives would be enriched.

WHY FORGIVENESS MATTERS

Forgiveness is in short supply yet blame surrounds us in abundance. Accusing others of wrongs is practically our new national pastime. It seems like everyone is being accused of something these days. It might be racism, sexism, homophobia, transphobia, or things that you may never have even heard of, such as colonialism and/or cultural appropriation.

This leads to the blame game. In the blame game, *appearing* to be the biggest victim is far more important than facts, much less any reasonable grievance standard. The blame game has also led to one of the hottest buzzwords in recent years, "Cancel Culture."

In short, if someone feels you have wronged them or committed the smallest act of insensitivity towards them, they will try to destroy your community standing, even your career, with an outraged mob summoned at a lightning clip (with the aid of social media). The response time for these misguided people truly is amazing—the minutemen who led to this country's founding would be put to shame. Now, imagine if our youth used all this energy for *good* instead of destroying someone for using the wrong pronouns!

Abetted by Cancel Culture, the blame culture is spiraling out of control. To keep the industry alive, victim-culture advocates now preach the concept of "microaggressions." Tiny slights, often unintended, they are said to supposedly ruin a victim's daily life. A corporate training document reviewed by the authors includes a typical example. A white male employee greets a black female worker in the morning before a busy workday and says, "I'm glad to see that you're on time and ready to roll this morning!" According to the blame game, this might be seen as a microaggression of both racism and sexism.

At this rate, we can't be far off from a new season of *CSI: Microaggressions Unit*. We can expect a *Thought Police* series to spin off next. Seriously though, the rise in blame culture tracks strongly with forgiveness' disappearance. This is especially troubling because what happens to a society without forgiveness is no mystery. History is replete with examples of where we're headed if we don't course-correct. Do The Salem Witch Trials ring a bell? How about China's Cultural Revolution?

A culture unable to forgive is divided. Its citizens become unrelenting, possessing a zero-sum mindset. People walk around with hardened hearts avoiding simple acts of kindness, no longer treating their peers with civility or respect. Think this is farfetched? Spend time in any big city. Or for a rural example, look up the heartbreaking story of the Hatfields and the McCoys.

THE BIBLICAL VIEW OF FORGIVENESS

We know we are fallen creatures. We may be made in God's image, but we are flawed and imperfect. We also know that when we sin, we sin more against God than our fellow man. Despite this, Jesus Christ forgave mankind for our sins. If God can forgive us, who are we not to forgive each other?

In fact, our relationships, both within the family and with coworkers, friends, neighbors, and casual acquaintances, afford us the best opportunities to practice being Christ-like. By accepting flaws and imperfections and forgiving trespasses as the Lord forgives ours, we can aspire to be more like the Lord.

Also, if we want *real* inclusiveness in our lives, <u>forgiveness</u> must be included. (The concept of inclusiveness need not only concern accepting different skin colors and other physical differences. It should extend to people who think and feel differently than us, and sometimes even clash with us.) As pastor and author A.W. Tozer quipped, "You've been forgiven. Act like it!" This truth is reflected in Jesus' teachings. He advises His followers on forgiveness after driving money changers from the temple in the Book of Mark, Chapter 11:

> "And whenever you stand praying, forgive, if you have anything against anyone, so that your Father who is in heaven will also forgive you for your offenses. But if you do not forgive, neither will your Father who is in heaven forgive your offenses. (Mark 11:25-26, NASB)"

FORGIVENESS MATTERS

Power of 4 comes together to improve as men, Christians, husbands, and fathers. Forgiveness is especially paramount in those last two categories. After all, relationships fray and crumble based on one's inability to forgive. None other than the incomparable pastor-teacher John MacArthur often discusses this concept on his *Grace to You* podcast. If you take one thing away from this book—besides our advice on running your own group—it should be to subscribe to this invaluable biblical resource.

During a show dedicated to forgiveness, MacArthur explained its importance to relationships. According to him, the inability to forgive not only destroys relationships, but it also decimates those in the relationship who don't forgive. MacArthur speaks extensively about those who forgive so that we may learn to do it better ourselves, describing their motives, actions, and characteristics. To illustrate this topic, he cites Paul's letter to Philemon, found in the Bible book of the same name. First, let's briefly run through that letter's story. While in a Roman jail, Paul met a slave named Onesimus who had stolen money from his master and run away. Paul converted him to Christianity but knew his young brother in Christ must return to Philemon to apologize.

The good news? Philemon was himself a Christian leader in the town of Colossae. Onesimus went back to his former master carrying a letter from Paul, preserved for us in the Bible. The letter is short, its message simple: Jesus Christ is the renewer of hearts. He had rehabilitated the hearts of Paul and Philemon, as well as Onesimus. As a man grateful to be saved by the forgiveness of Jesus, Philemon should in turn forgive his former slave's crimes.

MacArthur uses this short letter to illustrate several key points which we summarize below:

The Motives of One Who Forgives

MacArthur explains that Christians have several motivations to forgive others. The first is to recognize that we all owe a much larger debt to Jesus than any person who has wronged us. Speaking for the penniless slave, Paul says Philemon should put the bill on Paul's own tab. He isn't only speaking about money here. His larger point concerns the giant debt Philemon owes Paul for guiding him to God.

The second motivation is that by forgiving, Christians can be a blessing in others' lives. There is no higher expression of love than inspiring joy in others, especially when we are used to some being hard-hearted toward us. (Think about Ebenezer Scrooge's transition at the climax of *A Christmas Carol*.) Third, we are all called to be obedient to the Lord, and Jesus would certainly wish us to forgive those who commit minor trespasses against us.

The third characteristic is a concern for mutuality. As MacArthur explains, "If you're a Christian, you care about the fellowship. You care about the body of Christ, is what he's saying. You're concerned about others. You say, 'Look, I want to forgive you because I don't want chaos in the fellowship. I want harmony, I want peace, I want unity.'"

The Actions of One who Forgives

MacArthur believes forgiveness begins with *reception*, meaning opening your life back up to that person. Just as Paul asked Philemon to welcome his former slave as a fellow Christian, we must let a person who wronged us back into our lives, especially when they are ready to be back in our lives. Note: MacArthur is not advocating for allowing a practicing drug addict into your home. However, he believes that once they are clean, reception should occur.

The second action of forgiveness is restoration. This means bringing the person back into the fold to some degree. Summarizing Paul's message to Philemon, MacArthur says: "Don't you think perhaps that God had planned all along that when this man left you, he would come back in another way? He parted from you for a while that you should have him back forever. You lost a slave, and you gained a brother. God allowed it. God overruled it. A temporary separation to lead to an eternal relationship."

Restitution is forgiveness' third action. The person who wronged the other must make it right. This can take many forms, but it would have been tricky for Onesimus to repay Philemon since he was completely broke, and this occurred long before someone could be penniless and still hold a credit card.

Here, MacArthur counsels that sometimes Christians must

take the high road, graciously ignoring the need for restitution around worldly assets. He gives an example of what
you might say: "I know you were an ungodly sinful man and
I understand that behavior suited that kind of nature. Now
that you're a transformed person I no longer hold you responsible for that which you did in your unredeemed status.
I graciously forgive you." That would have been a wonderful
thing to do, and certainly would have been a Christian high
ground approach to the issue.

The Characteristics of One who Forgives
MacArthur also uses Paul's letter to Philemon to illustrate the
characteristics of those who forgive, which can be gleaned
from the early portions of the letter. Paul puts his trust in
Jesus Christ to protect the runaway slave he has converted.
Based on his faith, he also trusts Philemon, a Christian Paul
converted himself, who holds church services in his home.

Extrapolating from this, we can observe how someone willing to forgive has a concern for others. MacArthur describes
this as a love of choice, will, and self-sacrifice. Essentially, in
a hard world, Christians are expected to deeply care about
others, especially those repenting for past transgressions.

Now, let's discuss why we are so reluctant to forgive—especially men.

Reason Number One: We Don't Want to Appear Weak
As discussed, most of us are stuck playing roles, but there is
one role no man wants to play—the weakling. In our culture,
forgiveness is equated with weakness. We want to seem strong
by enacting justice, by chasing after vengeance.

The Bible tells us not to retaliate, but everything else
screams at us to punch back. Want examples? Pore through

Netflix or your own movie collection. You'll likely find a stash of movies centered on revenge. In fact, many action flicks, like *Payback, Ransom, The Terminator,* and *Hardcore* are like a steady cultural drumbeat with a simple message: "Men must take matters into their own hands—striking swiftly and violently."

Is it any wonder that we are in trouble when these are our totems? Now, for a real-world example. Consider the ongoing tragedy following the terror attacks of 9/11. America had the entire world on our side in the aftermath.

We *could* have pursued a peaceful resolution that may have nipped terrorism in the bud. Instead, we launched a permanent war that's killed thousands of Americans. A much higher number returned home wounded and/or dealing with psychological trauma. Additionally, millions are dead and/or displaced in the Middle East, not to mention, untold trillions of dollars were squandered on wars that did little besides make the world more unsafe. We don't mean to get all political with this point, but can any supporter of the War on Terror name a positive that came from it?

On a related note, scientists have studied the neurochemistry of revenge. Writing for the website Science of People, Vanessa Van Edwards describes a social experiment completed by researchers in Switzerland. They ran a game in their lab whereby players would betray one another, then be offered a chance at revenge against those who wronged them. All this intrigue occurred while players were hooked up to brain-monitoring equipment. The researchers noted how taking revenge lit up the reward centers of the brain. *Revenge felt good for the players.* Yet longer-term research shows revenge doesn't bring closure. Instead, it keeps us stuck in the event of being wronged, which MacArthur referred to as "picking at the scab."

Reason Number Two: The Entitlement Complex

It's obvious just how far America has strayed from its mindset of rights and responsibilities. Many of us now think in terms of privileges and entitlements. When we concentrate on what is "rightfully" ours, and maximizing our own sense of comfort, we stop caring about others.

Selfishness doesn't fit in with being our brother's keeper. Instead, dwelling on ourselves causes us to become atomized—divided as a people. Not only by a right-left politics paradigm, but we are also separated into many tiny little fiefdoms that don't collaborate or provide mutual aid. Trapped in this scenario, we are beholden to what we perceive to be our special interest. Tribalistic, we care little for others outside our immediate community, let alone any larger group or the greater good.

Power of 4 stands in stark contrast with this attitude. In fact, while working on this very chapter via an online meeting, Steve fell ill. Mark stopped what he was doing and contacted Steve's son and neighbor to ensure he was okay, getting the help he needed. This level of connectivity and community was once taken for granted in most American communities. Now it's a rarity.

Importantly, we aren't a bunch of old men shaking our fists at "those dern kids and their loud music." Entitlement and acting selfishly can be found within every generation and class within our culture, young or old. Carleton University psychology professor Janet Mantler has studied privilege in the workplace, finding it crosses age and generational barriers. To those adults who complain about youngsters being social media addicts, Mantler points out that "We're the ones responsible for all the texting. We made the phones."

Reason Number Three: We Run from Pain

Practically no one starts their day with sacrificing for others top-of-mind. Yes, there are some saints among us who *are* up at the crack of dawn devoting their lives to others, but they are outliers. Instead, most of us struggle to find the right mindset—not to mention, will—to devote ourselves to others, especially when we feel such pressure to get ahead in the rat race ourselves.

Tragically, our culture emphasizes selfish behavior, conspicuous consumption, and, above all else, personal gain. We all know how powerful peer pressure can be when we (or our kids) don't have fashionable sneakers, the latest gadgets, or an uncool haircut. Steve felt this kind of pressure decades before social media existed when he moved with his mom from rural Idaho to The Bay. A Martian could have fit in with the others better than young Steve did. Even in the '60s, a culture of avarice was alive and well, anticipating the selfie and extensive (digital) navel gazing that we now take for granted.

Giving back, as well as servant leadership, aren't things Americans are conditioned to aspire to. Instead, we're trained from birth to seek comfort and appeasement. We don't like to do things that feel bad or make us unhappy.

This is why Thoreau said people live lives of quiet desperation. Our big challenge is: "Why not?" *Why not take some risks? Why not be unquiet and help others through their struggles? Why not engage in a life of service to others?*

That last one is not easy but affords us the chance to enjoy a well-lived life, regardless of our circumstances. Possessing this kind of mindset, we can begin to control our circumstances, rather than allow them to control us.

Through it all, one thing is clear: If we want to turn around the negativity in modern society, we must practice forgiveness. Author Henry Cloud expounds on this in *Boundaries:*

When to Say Yes, How to Say No to Take Control of Your Life. As Cloud writes: "To forgive someone means to let him off the hook, or to cancel a debt he owes you. When you refuse to forgive someone, you still want something from that person, and even if it is revenge you want, it keeps you tied to him forever."

Power of 4 couldn't agree more. Our brotherhood helps brothers forgive by hastening the process. Having a group of men who you can be angry with, vent to, and who will listen patiently as you get stuff off your chest, allows you to begin the forgiving process faster than you otherwise would—if at all.

How We Helped Rodney

The day Rodney told us the sad tale of his failed partnership and friendship with Neil and Chris, we saw him relive emotions from that turbulent time. It was obvious to us all that he hadn't worked through his feelings completely. He may have *thought* he left this experience buried in his past, but it was still very much with him. A successful guy who had bounced back and done good things in his life, he was still trapped in time—clutching onto his anger, his disappointment.

After explaining the facts of what happened, Rodney turned to us, seeking advice. *What should he do?* Forgive Chris? Open up to his former friend to some degree? Demand restitution? He received feedback from a diverse collection of viewpoints that day, one of the primary benefits of Power of 4.

First, Steve put his therapist hat on. He pointed out how Chris didn't send an impersonal email or text. He showed up on Rodney's doorstep asking for nothing but forgiveness, in a way not unlike the story of Philemon. "That took guts," said Steve. "And it doesn't sound like he's trying to gain anything."

Mark was quick to speak up on that topic. He asked Rodney to speculate whether Chris was trying to sucker him into another bad deal of some sort. Mark said, "You can forgive someone without jumping back into bed with them. He burned you once and that's his fault. But if he burns you again it's yours." Once Rodney confirmed that nothing like that had happened, and especially given that he is in recovery, Mark advised Rodney to take his gesture sincerely.

Keith, like Steve, was impressed that Chris came for an in-person visit. "That's how it was done by previous generations, but here in Southern California—in these times? That shows character." In Keith's opinion, Chris was acting as a reformed man and deserved to be treated as such.

Ultimately, Rodney took the forgiveness path.

Soon after Power of 4, he reached back out to Chris, who had been in town for work. The two arranged to meet for dinner the next time he was in town. Chris sounded so relieved to reconnect that it brought a real feeling of positivity to Rod. He knew in his heart he was doing the right thing. The two men have since reconnected in a long-distance friendship, seeing each other when time and travel allows. Surprising themselves, they settled into the kind of relationship that they had before their partnership soured.

To this day, Rodney considers it one of the best things he ever did.

There's a postscript to this story. Chris eventually filled in Rodney on Neil's troubles and his prison sentence for fraud (due to later actions revealing the same treacherous pattern). Though Neil was the real villain in the story, Rodney wrote him a letter letting him know he was forgiven. In it he said he hoped Neil would leave jail a new man, willing to follow Christ. He never heard back, but had forgiven the man and made his peace, as the Bible teaches us.

* * *

It's time to change gears. In Part II, we will shift our book's format. We will present long-form stories from brothers highlighting the struggles they brought to the group and how Power of 4 helped them better cope with their challenges in a positive way. To protect identities, we again changed key details and names since these are not as important as the lessons the men received.

PART

STORIES

Just like the Bible instructs using parables, in this next portion we will offer narratives to demonstrate Power of 4's influence on men.

CHAPTER 7

Steve's Story: Come Ugly with a Blood Glucose Number

As cofounder of Power of 4 and its oldest brother, I have been elected by my friends and brethren to tell a personal story first. The other chapters in this section will include important tales from past brothers that illustrate important ways our brotherhood works together. We're changing names and details, so please, don't try to play detective and figure out who these tales belong to. Instead, pay attention to what's important—how our collective wisdom helped each brother.

For now, we are starting with my own narrative. It's a take on an old dog learning new tricks, and how I shifted my approach to Power of 4 after 18 years of meetings. This story also involves a brush with death that I recently experienced. Death isn't a fun subject, but it's nonetheless something that becomes more prominent in our minds as we age. Young people may feel invincible, but old folks know death is getting closer. I've sometimes pondered my own demise, a bit like the board game Clue my grandkids have played with me. In Clue, a death may come from being hit with a candlestick by Colonel Mustard in the library.

Crazy way to go, am I right? Weirder than that, I never would have expected that my own brush with mortality would be caused by . . . a strawberry milkshake. To properly tell the story of the killer strawberry milkshake, I must first give you a biographical sketch of my life. This is a condensed version from the book I recently published entitled *Never Alone: A Man's Companion Guide to Grief* (completed in 2021 with coauthor Michael Ashley).

This book documents my life, along with the journey I took through it with my beloved late wife Linda. It also explains how men can better deal with grief based on insights from my own feelings of loss following her death. I mention the book not only as an advertisement (You're reading one book I've written—try another!), but also because the completion of that book plays a pivotal role in my story.

A LITTLE BOY ALONE IN IDAHO

Although I've lived enough decades in California that most people assume I've been here since birth, that isn't the case. I was born in a rural community in Idaho. I didn't want to come out of the womb—I was born in the tenth month of my mother's pregnancy. (Even in my mother's tummy I must have suspected the rough family situation I would soon face and was in no hurry to experience it.)

I grew up believing I was my parent's third child, with an older brother and sister. In fact, I was the *fourth*, coming after a brother that was stillborn. As my mother matter-of-factly told me later, my birth was an ill-advised attempt to fix my parent's marriage after the stillbirth and other family problems.

No matter the circumstances, I was born to a dysfunctional family, embarking on a life that would often make me feel alone. My brother Dean is eight years older and very smart—he made a mint in the early days of the tech boom. But our age gulf meant we didn't spend much time together. My sister

Roberta is five years my senior and for years our relationship was quite stormy. When she was 18 and I was 13, I was the outgoing life of the party—leading people to assume I was the 18-year-old, and she was my younger sister. She resented that, of course, and it took time to dissipate lingering negativity between us.

Although there were bumps in the road with my siblings, the real problem was my relationship with my dad, Ellsworth Bagley. Dad was a railroad man. When I think back on my life with him, he was either away from home on a train, waiting by the phone for the next call from the station, or sleeping between shifts. He did have his good qualities; for example, he was an excellent dancer, but this didn't cause us to connect on a deeper level.

Our relationship was cold, and my mom didn't help. She worked a lot too. In fact, one of my earliest memories is sitting in our kitchen alone fixing myself a meal. Feeling alone is probably the single most common emotion of my childhood.

Life was an uphill battle for reasons beyond residing in an impossibly rural community. My teachers told my mom I was "slow" and would never read and write with any success. I wasn't slow by any means, but I did have a reading disorder long before teachers, especially those in rustic areas, were trained to spot such things and seek expert help. While my teachers might have suspected I would drop out of school and work on the railroad along with my dad, I was determined to show that there was nothing wrong with my ability to think. This led to the "Summer of Squanto" when I was nine.

Daily during the Summer of Squanto, I would walk down to a nearby church and spend the day reading a book from school entitled *Squanto: Friend of the Pilgrims*. As I would read, Pastor Mike, a visiting minister spending the summer in our tiny town, would be there to help me. Some days, I'd success-fully get through only one page. Other days I'd make blazing progress.

Other kids were swimming, climbing, and playing base-ball, but I was on a mission, one I achieved by summer's end. The doubt my teachers had in me would later become fuel to write my own book decades later. I even pondered trying to hand deliver them a copy, if any were still alive. I felt like I was on top of the world after mastering that book, but just a few years later my world would be shaken by the next big change. When I was 12, my mom told me she was divorcing my father.

This was stunning in a way that today's young people have trouble understanding. Many parents divorce these days, but in the late '50s it was quite a scandal, especially in our small town. I felt like just as I was getting everything together, it was being ripped apart again. That was the first bomb my mom dropped on me. The second was that we'd be moving to NorCal. I don't think calling me a fish out of water is quite strong enough.

CALIFORNIA LIVING AND MEETING LINDA

California was a huge change in many ways. My high school had more students than there were people in my hometown, and I was more alone than ever as my mom worked to sup-port us. Even though I felt adrift, I did what I always do—net-work, make friends, and find common interests. I got active in a nearby church and shortly thereafter devoted myself to my Lord and Savior Jesus Christ. Money was tight, but I could attend church camps and other events, thanks to parishio-ners who covered my costs.

I would soon head to Azusa Pacific University in SoCal.

That's where the next great event unfolded. I met Linda, the love of my life.

I loved her at first sight. I can remember it as clearly today as when I first glimpsed Linda back in '65. We were in the college gym in a big meeting of new students. I can recall even what she wore and her stirring testimony about putting her faith in Jesus Christ.

Being the confident young guy I was, my attempt to flirt with her failed. To make a long story short, I bungled it and didn't reconnect with her until senior year, at which point we began our true relationship. My early career involved working in churches as a pastor, both for youth and for the general congregation. At the same time, my marriage to Linda wasn't where I wanted it to be. We were both playing roles, like we've discussed in this very book, and it led to an unsatisfying union. For example, we had children together because we thought that's what a loving couple does.

It would take us many years to get to the bottom of our problems.

HELPING LINDA HEAL

After we had been married for some time, the awful truth of Linda's early life emerged. She had been sexually molested by different men, and the horrific crimes against her started as early as when she was a baby. Learning all this was hard, but it also unlocked Linda's true potential to love. It was ironic—many people feel their marriage loses it spark after decades together, but for us, that's when we found ours.

Linda and I found success as Christian counselors. She also became a dynamo of a speaker, bringing couples closer. One speaking tour we took in Japan stands out. Linda was only slotted to give a short talk at a few locations, but she was so engaging to the Japanese audience that the entire schedule was rearranged to make her the headliner. Linda found answers to many of the problems in her life. In turn, she helped thousands of couples improve their marriages. We enjoyed many great years together, but it all ended far too soon.

LIFE AFTER LINDA

My beloved wife Linda Bagley passed away in her sleep in the pre-dawn hours of Saturday, February 2, 2013. She had had heart trouble for years, and this is likely what claimed her life. In those first few days, my Power of 4 brothers were beyond critical. They kept me going while also serving as my emotional support network. They (and their wives) even ensured I was eating and resting. If not for them, I wouldn't have.

As I moved on from the loss of Linda, I found new purpose. I became more involved in my grandkids' lives and eventually resumed Christmas activities. Anyone who knew Linda knew that she was the queen of Christmas, and it was years before I could feel happy during the most wonderful time of the year.

Besides looking forward to participating in every Power of 4 meeting, I kept myself busy mentoring young men. For years, I also served in a leadership role for Arms of Love International, giving abandoned and abused children in Nicaragua and the Philippines a loving home. Long ago, Linda and I set a goal to cultivate a group of disciples. This work didn't stop with Linda's death. Ultimately, I've remained active and engaged thanks to my family, my Power of 4 brothers, and, of course, the good Lord.

In the years since Linda's passing, I kept thinking there ought to be a book to help men learn how to better grieve. Most of us don't do it well. Fearing vulnerability, we shut down and shut others out. This is to be expected in a society that also doesn't handle grief well. Instead of preparing us for this unavoidable moment, our culture promotes an unrealistic—and unhelpful—view that we will live forever.

At some point, my thinking changed from wishing there was a book on the subject to deciding I needed to write *the* book on the subject. I won't lie—I also felt I had something to prove to those teachers who called me slow. Despite having a long career in the church and in counseling, I knew being a published author would be the ultimate proof that those teachers were wrong about me. With this top-of-mind, I began the long process of collecting notes, thinking about how to capture key events, and interviewing friends and family. I found a coauthor, named Michael Ashley, who helped bring my story to life. Now, the real meat of my story, what you're here to read, is what happened *after* we finally completed my book, *Never Alone*.

THE KILLER MILKSHAKE

In late 2021 I was ready to celebrate!

I had completed my final review of all 22 chapters of *Never Alone* and handed a few minimal edits back to Michael. My part in the book was essentially done. Next it would be handed off to Claudine Mansour, our talented designer, who would turn our manuscript into a real book for publishing. I was elated for a few reasons. First, I had accomplished one of my "bucket list" goals. Second, and more importantly, the story of my life and my relationship with Linda would now be documented, serving as a guide for other men struggling with loss.

When I say I handed a few edits to Michael, I mean literally. This wasn't me shooting off an email or even sending a FedEx package. We met in person to celebrate the end of the writing process. Michael had moved from SoCal to my home state of Idaho but was in town for business, so we marked our accomplishment by gathering for a victory lunch. (Victory may sound odd when we're talking about something like penning a book, but, believe me, it's a long haul as difficult as any sporting event, so victory *is* quite a reasonable term to use in my estimation.)

Michael is a down-to-earth guy like me. We didn't meet in some posh Italian eatery or a trendy Laguna Beach joint where you might run into a celebrity—we enjoyed our victory at good old IHOP. Poring over the menu, I couldn't help but be drawn to the strawberry milkshake. It seemed like the perfect beverage to honor the occasion, the ideal substitute for champagne.

That strawberry milkshake made me feel like a kid all over again. It increased the pleasure I felt over finishing the book. It seemed like the ideal way to honor the milestone, and I drained that sucker down to the bottom. (Michael said when the waitress brought it that there was no way I could possibly finish it, but I proved him wrong. I downed the whole glass and wished there was a little more left.)

Our business concluded; we took my car to the airport so Michael could make his flight. I thanked him for making the project possible before dropping him off at John Wayne Airport. Then I turned my car towards home, still riding the high of my victory and, of course, that delicious strawberry milkshake.

That's when my world turned upside down.

MY LOST WEEKEND

Driving home Friday, I was looking forward to some peace and solitude. I would have at least four days with the house to myself because my roommates were out of town. I planned to read, go on walks, and work on various tasks I had put off while finishing the book project. Unfortunately, none of those activities occurred.

The rest of Friday I felt off. I wasn't thinking straight. I lost my glasses which I hadn't done in about 20 years. I also misplaced my medicine box, so I wasn't taking the medications I take daily. I felt fuzzy, like you sometimes do if you are awakened in the middle of the night and are suddenly expected to think logically at your normal level. At some point I eventually drifted off, figuring I'd be back up to speed come Saturday.

The next morning wasn't much better.

My head was still foggy. Worse, now I felt weak. Knowing I needed to keep my energy up, I drove to a nearby smoothie shop. Their delicious drinks have become my go-to pick-me-up in recent years. The smoothie didn't help my energy level, but the cold liquid did aggravate my asthma. Still feeling lousy, now I was coughing up phlegm. I clearly remember planning to head home to read, but by the time I got there, I had completely forgotten that idea. I think I just puttered around the house for a while.

I don't remember Saturday too well, but it's still clearer than Sunday.

As far as I can piece together, I slept almost the entire day. I don't remember eating anything, talking to anyone, or doing anything outside the bedroom. I didn't get any calls I can remember, but that isn't unusual. No one knew I was alone or had any special reason to check on me. Without a doubt, I was growing weaker and more confused by the hour.

My next clear memory came on Monday, when God and a good doctor teamed up to save my life.

NEEDED INTERVENTION

I woke up Monday feeling sicker and weaker. One blindingly clear thought forced itself to my consciousness. I must go to the lab for a fasting blood test to detect diabetes. I had been on the bleeding edge of *full-blown* diabetes for about a decade. I was taking some medication and (badly) following a diet to control it. The test was meant to measure how well I was managing my diabetes without getting more serious treatment.

Although I didn't feel great, I knew I had to keep the appointment at all costs. In my counseling practice it was a great annoyance when people no-showed for their appointments, so I've always avoided doing that to other professionals. After the test, the technician said they would send the results to my physician, Dr. Muhammed Ali, to review the next day. (Dr. Ali is a great guy who cares about his patients and likes to introduce himself by saying, "I'm Dr. Muhammed Ali. But don't worry, I don't box!") I chuckled at his joke the first time, knowing he's way too young to have even seen his namesake fight.

After the blood test I headed home. Fixated on increasing my energy level, I again hit the smoothie shop. It didn't make me feel any better, so the rest of Monday had more in common with Sunday than even Saturday. Except for two brief stops at the smoothie place, the folks at the blood test facility were the only people I had talked to since Friday morning.

That would all change in the middle of the night.

Tuesday at 1:00 a.m. I was startled awake by my phone ringing. I had no idea of the time, or even where I was, so I answered it in utter confusion. A concerned voice came through the receiver: "Mr. Bagley, this is Dr. Muhammed Ali. I couldn't sleep so I decided to review your test results."

"The boxer?" I answered in a befuddled voice. I must have been out of it.

"This is your *doctor*, Mr. Bagley. You're in serious trouble. You must act. *Now.* Your blood sugar came back at 515—I suggest you call 911 and get to the hospital immediately."

"But I'm feeling okay, and I really need to be here 'til the kids wake for school. I'll come to your office after they're on the bus," I said. (I was so out of it I thought my children—who now have children of their own—were sleeping in the next room and had school in the morning.)

The next thing I knew it was 4:00 a.m. and I was still sitting on my bed in the same position I was in when I spoke to Dr. Ali. I was so confused and weak I hadn't moved and didn't know what was going on. His words bounced around in my head: "Get to the hospital."

Sidenote: If you want to know the best time to go to the ER and not find a waiting room full of sick people, it's 4:00 a.m. The place was deserted, and a bunch of nurses flew into action upon seeing me. Apparently, I was able to tell them my blood sugar level because they immediately put me on monitors, giving me a shot to reduce my blood sugar.

I also know I was still terribly confused, as I told them I live alone with no support network. None of that's true. My daughter Stefani luckily was able to straighten out many misconceptions when she arrived soon after. While I was in the ER, Dr. Ali called me again. Relieved, he was glad to hear I was in the hospital. Over a three-way call with the ER docs and him, we made plans for me to go to his office as soon as they discharged me.

As soon as I was home, friends and loved ones showed up to visit. The whole Power of 4 was there with wives in tow, giving me their strength in my time of need. One of them even ordered a humidifier for my house to keep me comfortable, and all of them committed to helping in any way possible.

The opposite of being alone, it was touching and made me feel cared for.

I was also visited by a diabetes specialist while still at the hospital. She explained that when your blood sugar is above 500, there's a high risk of slipping into a sugar coma, resulting in death. Mine had been a whopping 515, so I came close to the edge. She also said my sugar was likely in the 250 range when I felt so weak and foggy on Saturday. (For reference, 100 to 120 is the ideal target.) I knew I had work to do to get my body and blood in shape.

But let's be clear about one thing: If the good Lord had not reminded me about that blood test, I would likely be dead. If Dr. Ali had gotten to my blood sugar test results sometime during Tuesday, I would likely be dead. God and a good doctor saved my life, and I take that very seriously. In other good news, by changing my diet and other behaviors, I dropped my blood sugar to 125 (just above normal) within ten days. But what if things didn't play out so favorably? My family, friends, and brothers would have stood over my grave, and if someone asked them how I perished, they'd be forced to say, "He drank that entire killer strawberry milkshake."

Praise be to God this didn't occur. Still, I had to make up a lot of ground with my family and with Power of 4. I had just put all of them through hell.

WHAT POWER OF 4 HAD TO SAY

My first meeting back, it was clear I'd be the major topic of discussion. A brother named Kevin kicked things off by leading a prayer thanking God for me getting the care I needed.

Mark then asked me to tell the story of the killer milkshake as I have here. Then, our normal style of discussion began.

Another brother named Nick asked me point blank: "Steve, why didn't our brotherhood know you've been battling diabetes or pre-diabetes for the last decade?"

Mark chimed in next. "You've been coming to Power of 4 meetings for nearly 20 years. You've talked about asthma and other troubles, why not this?" I told them what I believed to be the truth: "I didn't think my health concerns should be a burden. Until that milkshake, I thought I had things under control."

Nick looked at me with a stern look that also showed deep caring. "Steve, if you call *that* control, remind me to never catch a ride in your car. On a serious note, isn't it clear health concerns are important? We've helped brothers with weight loss. We've supported each other through cancer scares and all kinds of other things . . . but diabetes doesn't count?"

I couldn't argue that point. "I agree. My health is important for you guys to know about. It's doubly crucial because I'm our oldest member. But the main thing I learned is I don't want to put my family, you, my brothers, and all my friends through that nightmare again."

Mark continued, "Steve, let's walk through how the weekend would have been different if your health was an open topic with Power of 4. First, we would've known you were going to be alone for four days, so we'd have been sure to check in with you. Second, we would've known your blood sugar was a concern, so we'd be in the habit of—at a minimum—texting you to get your count. Third, if we didn't hear from you, we'd have been at your house Saturday night."

"Doesn't that sound like a better plan than going to the ER at 4:00 a.m.?" teased Nick.

Again, I had to admit it all made sense. My silence and my lack of prioritizing my health almost got me killed by a strawberry milkshake, of all things. But I was about to get a startling piece of feedback that told me I had a lot more to think about than I already had going through my mind.

Kevin, with a kindly tone, started to ask me about the book I had just finished. He said, "So, on Friday you met your co-author on *Never Alone*. You've talked about this book many times and have been working on it for a long time. Didn't you tell me all your conversations were turned into notes?"

I didn't know where he was going with this, but I answered anyway: "Yes, we had many hours of interviews, and that was turned into more than 250 pages of manuscript, including additional content. Why are you asking?"

Kevin replied, "So, in all of that book, am I correct in guessing you didn't mention even once that you're fighting diabetes?"

I was dumbfounded. Kevin was right! An entire book about my life, including several chapters about my later years, and diabetes hadn't come up once. The others could see the shock on my face. All I could say was, "Wow. You're correct. I've buried this health concern from everyone, including *myself.* I'm going to do better, and I hope you all will accept my apology for hiding this from you."

Mark was quick to pull things back. "Now hang on. This isn't a blame game or an apology tour. You don't need to say you're sorry for anything you've done. You want to do better in the future, and we want to support you, to help you better deal with your health challenges."

"It sounds like you already have some action items, and all of us look forward to helping you out," Nick added.

That made me feel a lot better. These men, *my brothers,*

all of whom I had inconvenienced—not to mention, fright-ened—by not coming ugly about my health, didn't hold a grudge towards me. I sometimes think of diabetes as being betrayed by my own blood cells, but I know my Savior will never turn against me. Neither will Power of 4.

STEVE BAGLEY'S DEFINITION OF FRIENDSHIP

Jesus set the standard when He called us His friends and said a friend could be closer than a brother. The Son of God leaving Heaven to hang out with us—what a mind-blowing idea! Being with those twelve men for three years served Je-sus' intentional strategy to develop followers so they could witness His teachings and actions. He didn't choose to marry, nor to raise children. Instead, Jesus' overriding purpose was to demonstrate a holy life of love, ending in His sacrificial death.

The events during that period repeatedly demonstrated the commitment Jesus had to their brotherhood. My like-minded spiritual friends (both men and women) are my fam-ily, my soul bonded to brothers and sisters in Jesus. When a brother is in my "friend circle," I want to be there for him. One of my highest commitments is to show up for him, to feed him. It's also to trust him, to pay attention to him. Like-wise, I am always ready to forgive him, encourage him, ask God's blessings to fill his life, enjoy his company, and laugh together as often as we can.

The good things deep friendship brings are not unlike peanut butter. When you smear it on a sandwich your fingers get sticky. The more sandwiches you make for your friends, the more peanut butter you get on yourself. Ultimately, I want to be knuckle-deep in peanut butter (friendship) every day. And not in milkshakes—even of the strawberry variety.

In our next chapter, we will tell the story of how Power of 4 helped one of our brothers with a challenging family situation. Like many parents who send their kids off to college these days, he struggled to understand the daughter who returned. One who now identified as a lesbian and questioned her gender.

CHAPTER 8

Greg's Story: A Daughter Working on a Ph.D. in Confusion

Some of the most challenging issues brought to Power of 4 are family problems. Life is full of ups and downs, but the downs are especially hurtful when they involve our loved ones, our children most of all. Most dads recognize that even if our kids will always remain those little beings we loved with all our hearts in their youth, as they age, they become their own people. We can still love them unconditionally, but our ability to exert control over them drops off dramatically.

Still, even when our sons and daughters become full-fledged grownups, when they run into trouble, it hurts us in deep and profound ways we didn't know we could hurt. Maybe this is the same feeling Jesus Christ experiences when we stumble and fall ourselves. This chapter's tale captures the pain and uncertainty fathers feel when their children start making bad decisions. Sometimes when this happens, we don't even recognize our own kids anymore, but still, we try to help them as best as we can.

In this case, Power of 4's mission was to provide support for our brother as he navigated a serious situation—that's still unfolding to this day. To be sure, the rulebook has yet to be penned on how to deal with the many startling problems America's youth face in these strange and dark times.

We truly wish there was because, as anyone who's paying attention to the news knows, an already bad situation is fast escalating into a full-blown crisis. The good news? We have the Bible to guide us and Power of 4 for support.

Now to our story. It comes from a past brother named Greg. Like nearly all our brethren, he left on good terms, in his case a family move. Over the years, we've kept in touch. We support him from afar, especially as he's gone on to form a group loosely based on Power of 4 in his new state of Texas.

We asked Greg's permission to share his story, which he readily provided. We've changed names and details to preserve his family's privacy, but the key to this narrative isn't in the minutia. It's in the trouble Greg experienced as a father and a man. How Power of 4 helped him cope with his dilemma is also paramount. As with Steve's story, we will begin at the *beginning*, this time with Greg's upbringing in small-town America.

WHY, A LITTLE OIL UNDER THE FINGERNAILS NEVER HURT NO ONE

Most everyone knows the Texas Panhandle, the rectangular spot that's easy for kids to draw compared to the Lone Star State's other borders. Not everyone is as familiar with its next-door neighbor, the *Oklahoma Panhandle*. This narrow land strip is where Greg was born. A barren area, Steve has commented before how Greg is the only brother in Power of 4 history to give him a run for his money on growing up in the most rural of areas.

Rural is one word for the locale Greg emerged from. Another is desolate. Ravaged by drought and depression in the early days of this country, it has since been undone by mass exodus as residents fled to other states in later decades.

Today, the population of several panhandle counties is lower than it was in 1907. How many other places can you say that about in America, besides Detroit?

Long before Greg was a twinkle in his Daddy's eye, the Oklahoma Panhandle went by other monikers. It was once known as "No Man's Land." Greg took that name to heart, aware he was growing up in the middle of nowhere, somewhere he didn't quite belong.

Although rural living was all he knew as a boy, he could recognize that where he lived was *different* than the America shown in the movies. For one thing, no outsiders ever (willingly) came to town. Later in life, Greg burst out laughing in the theater when he took his kids to see the Pixar movie *Cars*. The dying little town they're all so desperate to save reminded him that much of home.

Of course, there is *one* reason people do stay in the Panhandle. Oil was all Greg knew growing up. Oklahoma is a major U.S. petroleum source and has been for some time. It was certainly the raison d'être for Greg's hometown. Everyone worked in the oil fields or served to support those who did; for instance, supplying equipment or maintaining the machines for drilling and/or extracting oil from the earth. Likewise, the scarce number of restaurants and motels existed for the same reason: servicing men working the fields.

Drilling for oil is dirty, exhausting work, which Greg saw firsthand daily. His dad was an oil man, and his oldest brother took a job as an apprentice right out of high school. Daily, the two returned with dust and oil coating every pore of their skin. They'd spend a small eternity trying to rub themselves clean. Only a real oil man can never get all that grime off.

Still years away from working on a dangerous rig himself, little Greg found oil had other ways of creeping into his life. In the Oklahoma Panhandle, oil is ubiquitous, like how sand gets into everything when you live by the beach. As a teen, Greg felt the oil hung in the air like a haze, making his hair greasy, staining the buildings around him.

He remembers once when he got a splinter, and his dad went to work it out with his fingernail. Greg recoiled from the sight of oil under his fingernail. "Dad, stop! Your fingernail's dirty." His dad only looked at him with amusement. "You call that dirty? Why, a little bit under the fingernails never hurt no one. You'll know that truth soon enough when you join us in the fields." Then he dug the splinter out over Greg's continuing protests.

Greg realized from this that his dad just assumed he'd also join the family business. 14-year-old Greg couldn't imagine anything worse. He already felt like a fish out of water. He loathed the thought of being a fish out of water coated in sticky, dirty oil. Apprehensive and fearful, he dreaded his fate. Luckily, he had a relative who understood his plight—and wished to help.

GRANDPAP AND THE YANK

As soon as Greg entered high school, he began underachieving. Concerned, his teachers communicated their confusion to his parents. They all knew Greg had brains. He could do much better than he was—if only he applied himself.

Greg didn't see the point. If he was going to grind it out as a wildcat driller in some oil field, why bother analyzing *Othello* in English class or puzzling through algebra? It didn't make a difference. His destiny was sealed. Still, his parents appealed to his duties and responsibilities to himself. Their entreaties fell on deaf ears.

Things went on this way for the first few months of school until a fishing trip changed the course of Greg's life. His grandfather, whom he called Grandpap, showed up unannounced early one Saturday morning. "Fetch your fishing tackle," he told Greg. "We're heading out."

Journeying on Grandpap's boat was one of life's great pleasures, so Greg needn't be told twice. Sometimes these excursions were planned weeks in advance, during which time Greg would picture catching bass after bass. (This was thanks to his grandfather's near mystical ability to pinpoint the best locales.) Other days, like this one, Grandpap would just show up out of the blue and they'd hit whatever hot spot had been identified.

Today was about something more than catching fish. As soon as they got into open water, Grandpap laid his cards on the table. "Greg, I spent my working life in the oil fields. It put a good roof over our heads. It made sure we never went without. Your daddy spends his days out there. It's treated him good. Same's true for your brother. But you. You're different, ain't you?"

Greg froze. He hadn't anticipated this talk. No more calm lake and enjoyable day for him. Things had gotten uncomfortable fast, or they stood to. That's because he would never dream of lying to his grandfather. A kindly old man, he still sported wrists bigger than Greg's calves, and was no one to fool with.

Greg dreaded saying anything to displease him. "I, uh . . . I just don't feel it's right for me."

"A career in oil isn't?"

This wasn't getting easier. Better to get it over with. "To tell you the truth, I hate oil. I really do. The thought of working in it every day *forever* makes me . . ."

"Makes you depressed?"

Greg didn't know if he would say it that way, but it was close. "I'm sorry."

Grandpap took a while to respond. In the expanding stillness he reeled in one line to check the bait then recast it. "You ain't cut out for it. That's just it."

Greg reddened.

"There's no shame in that, boy. Better to figure things out now rather than years later. But you must find out what you're meant to do."

"Yes, sir."

"Now, why aren't you trying hard at school?"

Greg explained his rationale—that it wouldn't make any difference if he got A's or F's. He'd end up with the same life.

Grandpap grinned. "You're half right. You *don't* need an education to live here. But if you ever hope to turn things around, if you ever hope to leave . . ." Greg sat up at once. Grandpap smiled, knowing the effect he was producing. " . . . then getting an education *is* the only way to do it." He added, "You have a brain. You get that from my side. Now use it. Or this is our last fishing trip."

Greg knew it wasn't smart to argue, but he was also confused. "Grandpap, I've seen boys join the army then come home to work in the fields years later. I've seen guys go off to college and come back to work in the oil fields. Only wearing a tie. What can I do differently?"

His grandfather leaned in close so Greg wouldn't mistake his next words. "If you study and have faith in the Lord, the path will become obvious. And I've an idea to get you started. I want you to call on Mr. Green tomorrow."

On a day full of surprises, Greg was shocked yet again. "The Yank?"

"He can help you learn about jobs that don't involve you getting covered in oil."

"What will I say when I go over there?"

Grandpap patted his hand. "Don't worry. I've talked to him about it already. He's expecting you."

Overwhelmed, Greg didn't know what to say.

"You're welcome, boy. But I do feel about talked out on this subject. How about we catch some fish now?"

Turns out, Greg's grandfather had set him up to work for one Dr. James Green, the medic who ran the town's only chiropractic practice. (In fact, the only clinic like it anywhere for 200 miles.) He was known to most of the town as "the Yank" because he had moved there from Boston—and people migrating to rural Oklahoma from *anywhere* else was unheard of. This man would play a big role in shaping who Greg became, but in the beginning, he was just the boss.

WHAT GREG LEARNED FROM THE OUT-OF-TOWNER

Greg spent his high school years toiling in Dr. Green's clinic. This wasn't just a matter of pushing a broom or answering calls. Dr. Green also reviewed Greg's coursework between patient visits. As he told Greg, "If you ever want to get out of here, you'll need excellent marks."

Between his demanding boss and the fear of disappointing Grandpap, Greg wasn't going to argue. His grades turned around at once as he combined his natural intelligence with a newfound dedication to learning.

As he got to know Dr. Green, their relationship became friendlier. Greg worked up the courage one day to ask him why he had moved from the East to a backwards little town in the Oklahoma Panhandle.

Dr. Green smiled in his kind way. "There was an accident."

"An accident?"

"I'll spare you the details. But afterwards, I needed a scenery change."

Greg didn't catch his meaning, so Dr. Green explained. "It's like this. Either I was to hit the bottle hard and never stop—or get the hell out of the city. I chose option number two."

Greg had never heard such a frank admission from an adult. It puffed him up with pride but left him tongue-tied. He didn't want to spoil Dr. Green's confidence in him by saying something dumb. "I see, sir," was what he settled on. Then the two went back to work.

In time, Greg learned more about the chiropractic business than just how to ring up customers. Dr. Green patiently taught him how to review a chart and how to care for patients, diving deeper into anatomy and chemistry, the latter a subject he had always favored in school. Greg began to wonder if he, too, could become a healer like his mentor.

Later, he would reflect on these years as the best education he ever could have hoped for. His senior year, Greg shared the news with his family that he was applying to universities in Oklahoma and Texas to study medicine. He was nervous going in, but it was clear his parents admired his choice. "I'm proud of you," Grandpap also told him, filling him with satisfaction.

Even so, as a realist at 18, Greg knew his family couldn't give much towards his education. But he had a plan for that. Between his strong grades and completing endless scholarship applications, he thought he could pull something together. A month later he got the news he dreamed about. A Texas university had not only accepted Greg into its premed program, but provided him with a scholarship covering tuition, room & board, and even textbooks.

Without delay, he rushed down to tell Dr. Green the good news. The man blinked back tears. "You've been like a son to me," he told Greg. "I hoped from the day you walked in you'd achieve something like this."

"You don't care that I'm going to be an M.D., not a chiropractor?"

"It's your life." Mr. Green shook his head. "My advice to you is this: Even as you escape this small town, remember the good things about this place, not just the not-so-pretty stuff. Remember the country people who worship God and take care of their own."

"I will, sir."

Then Dr. Green surprised Greg by promising him a monthly stipend if he kept his grades up, bridging the final bit of expense the young man needed.

Greg took Dr. Green's advice. He never forgot the virtues of rural Oklahoma, even as he moved on to bigger and better things. In fact, Dr. Green and Grandpap were still on his mind years later when he ran into unexpected problems with his own children.

This is where the story he told Power of 4 begins.

WHAT COLLEGE CAN DO TO A YOUNG ADULT THESE DAYS

Fast forward a few decades.

Greg is now a successful oncologist living and working in SoCal. Coming out of college with excellent grades, he found his knack as a cancer specialist. His work in chemotherapy has been recognized by his peers nationally because, beyond seeing patients, he also publishes peer-reviewed articles in academic journals. Dr. Greg, as we will call him henceforth, became so revered in the medical sector that people all over the world now come to see him upon being diagnosed with cancer.

At the same time his career flourished, Greg managed to raise three children alongside his beloved wife Karen. They first had a son named Allen, then a daughter named Samantha, and finally another son Alex. They are all three years apart, leading to a little ribbing from Dr. Greg's friends: "That's how they do it in Oklahoma—like clockwork."

Joking aside, the family remained tight. The children were raised with strong ties to the Christian faith and a special emphasis on the importance of education. College wasn't even a question for Dr. Greg's kids. It was a natural step on the way to adulthood. All of them got the speech from Dad at some point on what learning had already done for their family.

Allen headed off to school first. He chose a private college on the East Coast, famous for its business program, and, like his dad, received a sizable scholarship paying his way there. He graduated with stronger conservative values and deeper ties to Christianity than he had when he enrolled.

To Dr. Greg's admiration, his wise son recognized the hypocrisy and victim culture of the woke activists on campus and rebuffed their message. As he told his dad: "These kids are far richer than me. They wouldn't be caught dead living in our house or driving my car, yet they tell me *my family and my religion* are the real problem? I told 'em complain to their au pair, not their classmates."

The way Allen stayed committed to his values in college buoyed Dr. Greg and his wife. They hoped Samantha would enjoy a similar positive experience when she went off to school. Instead, it went all wrong.

Like Dr. Greg, Samantha favored the healing profession. She chose to study psychology with an interest in becoming a social worker, gaining admission to a medium-sized Christian school in the South. Ironically, her education was *anything* but Christ-centered. After just one semester, she appeared cold and distant when she came back to visit. More troublingly, she refused to attend church except for a Christmas service which she went to at Karen's insistence.

Dr. Greg thought she was just struggling to adjust to college life. He couldn't have been more off-base. Heading into her sophomore year, Samantha transformed radically. She cut off her long hair, an almost unthinkable move for a girl who always took pride in her looks. Her remaining locks she dyed purple. Meanwhile her wardrobe changed overnight to feature lots of black numbers and T-shirts pushing feminist slogans.

Samantha was suddenly an angry young woman with a surly boyfriend named Jason, who acted openly hostile to her parents. Her behavior continued to change in frightening ways. For one thing, Dr. Greg noticed how Samantha's friends on social media often referred to her as just "Sam" in their posts.

This puzzled him. All her life Samantha hated being called Sam. She used to punch her brothers if they called her that, always using either her full name or the more feminine-sounding "Sami."

The next time Samantha visited home, Dr. Greg quizzed her about the name change, also bringing up her hair style—shorter than ever. Trying not to sound accusatory, he asked, "What's going on? For almost 20 years you've hated being called Sam. Now it's what all your friends call you on Instagram?"

Dr. Greg had no idea he was walking into a minefield. Meanwhile, Samantha looked peeved to have to explain herself. "Dad, you remember Jason? Well, Jason's gone. I'm with Joyce now."

Dr. Greg was struggling to keep up without a spreadsheet. "Joyce? Is that a guy or a girl?"

Samantha rolled her eyes. "A girl, obviously. Haven't you been listening?"

"So, you dumped Jason . . . to be with a woman?"

Samantha crossed her arms. "I didn't dump 'Jason' at all."

Dr. Greg was stumped. He truly wasn't following and didn't want to risk more ire. "Wait. Are you saying Jason became a girl . . . named Joyce?"

Samantha sighed. "Um, that's an incredibly uneducated way to explain it, but, yes, Joyce is a woman who's left the deadname of Jason behind. Just as *she* found herself, *I* am finding myself. I may be a lesbian named Samantha, or I may be a transgender man named Sam. I'm exploring my identity with the help of a caring community, and there's nothing you can do to stop me."

Dr. Greg felt like someone had just run him over. The whole thing was incomprehensible. His lovely daughter had turned into some goth feminist. No that wasn't it. She had morphed into a lesbian *with the same boyfriend as before.* And now she was trying to tell him that she might be a man?

He couldn't process the facts before him. All he could do was say, "The rules are still the same in this home. No drugs or funny business. You seem lost, but your mom and I'll help you find yourself if you let us."

Samantha stormed out without another word.

Dr. Greg felt consumed by his daughter's problems in the days to come. When his youngest son Alex got wind of Samantha's changing personality, he tried consoling his father. "Dad, don't worry about me. When I go to college, I'll be the same kid like Allen was. This isn't your fault."

Dr. Greg wished he could agree. As he struggled with raw emotions like anger and sadness, he turned to Power of 4.

HOW WE HELPED GREG

Power of 4 hears all kinds of stories. There are work challenges, personal tales of codependency, and, of course, plenty of family issues. Even so, Greg's story shocked us all. We all knew Samantha as a beautiful young woman with long brown hair. Greg had to actually share some of her recent social media posts so we could see firsthand her transformation into "Sam." Obvious to the group was the that fact Greg was hurting terribly and taking all the blame.

Steve shared his thoughts first. "Greg, I've counseled people who've suffered from the most messed up childhoods you can imagine, and it wrecked their lives. So, let's get this out of the way. Did you ever abuse Samantha? Did you ever make her feel unloved or treat her as less than your boys?"

Greg was hot. "Of course not! You know how I raised her."

"Okay. Okay." Hands up, Steve tried to talk him down. "Don't get upset. Of course, I knew the answer was no. You gave her an ideal upbringing centered on family and church. There's nothing you could have done better, so you must recognize this situation isn't because of *you*. You didn't cause this. Karen didn't either."

Mark went next: "Greg, one of the difficult things I picked up from your story is that a Christian college, of all places, contributed to Samantha's problems—enabling, even supporting her behavior in ways. You must feel betrayed that a Christian institution led her away from Christ."

Dr. Greg nodded. "You're right. It's crazy. Allen went to a school without religion and somehow came out a stronger Christian than ever, but my little girl went to a Christian college and became someone I don't even recognize."

Nick jumped in at this point. "Samantha will always be your little girl, but she's a thinking person that's on her own now.

If you try to force anything on her, or push her apart from this jerk of a boyfriend—girlfriend—whatever—she has, how do you think she'll take it?"

Dr. Greg recognized the wisdom in what Nick said. "Hmm. She'd no doubt rebel even harder, although that's hard to believe. She seems fixated on this guy/girl, and they are manipulating her. (I can't believe I am saying this.) I just wish I didn't feel so powerless."

Andrew had something important to say next. "Greg, you *aren't* powerless in this situation. You can pray for her to find her way. This guy is a scumbag, and the college is filling her head with garbage, but both will fail in the long run. It's up to you to be the last man standing for her."

Sizing up the pain on his brother's face, Andrew continued with sympathy, "Greg, your daughter's actions don't reflect on your character. Or your faith. They reflect on hers, but she's young and she still has time to find her way back to the path. You need to focus on being a supportive and loving dad while making it clear you don't support the choices she's making. If you don't want to lose her, she must know *you* are her lifeline, as you always have been. More than anything, don't forget where you came from—maybe it'll help her remember where she came from, too."

Andrew's wisdom struck Dr. Greg. As he told us later, it was the kind of advice Dr. Green might have given him in the Oklahoma Panhandle. It was what he needed, delivered by new mentors in his life—his brothers in Christ.

After venting some more with Power of 4, Dr. Greg began assessing the situation with the same analytical mind that brought him such professional accolades. Over many months, he began formulating a plan to support his daughter without playing into the poisonous ideology causing her to make such disastrous life choices.

POWER OF 4 AND DR. GREG

The conversation with Dr. Greg captured in this chapter was the first of many held across several meetings. We would often discuss a part of the "Samantha Situation," chipping away at facts instead of treating the problem as an overwhelming whole. Every Power of 4 brother pitched in to help Dr. Greg. (This meant reading up about sexuality because we were at a disadvantage dealing with a problem full of buzzwords we'd never heard of.)

Still, Power of 4 often brought new information to the table, such as research on the sexual fluidity of teen girls, and the fact that they are more susceptible to peer pressure regarding their orientation and their gender. We also helped Dr. Greg spot signs of psychological problems in his daughter.

Realizing that she fit many of the criteria of depression, Dr. Greg used his medical connections to locate a therapist in her college town that would not just feed into her claims of transgenderism. The therapist reported progress and Samantha was undeniably brighter on her next visit home. In fact, *home* became an important place for Dr. Greg to interact with his daughter.

Committed to the process, Dr. Greg and his wife also set down ground rules for Samantha during her summer breaks and other trips back. First, she'd be addressed as Samantha or Sami. Second, she'd be expected to treat her parents and brothers with respect. Third, Jason or Joyce or whatever name her boyfriend chose to use would not be welcome in their home. Samantha readily agreed to these rules—even the last one. To her credit, she followed them whenever she was home.

Dr. Greg's relationship with his daughter also benefitted

from the fact that he learned not to take the blame for her actions. He made it clear he didn't approve of her behavior, yet still loved her and always would. As the group advised him, Dr. Greg became the pillar in her life that was there for her when she was ready—even if he refused to cater to her whims.

Throughout this harrowing process, Dr. Greg learned much about himself too. As he later admitted to Mark, he waited too long to come to the group with his situation. The lesson Dr. Greg took from his months of brotherhood is that *no* problem should be shouldered by one man alone, especially when he has a support system. Based on all this support, he was able to make wiser decisions and be a better dad after unburdening himself.

The latest update on Dr. Greg's story surfaced when Steve recently checked in with his friend and brother. "Here's the big news," Steve told us. "Samantha broke up with Jason/Joyce after a domestic violence incident resulting in the boyfriend being locked up."

"What happened?" asked Keith.

"A surprising thing. A surprisingly *good* thing. At 1:30 a.m., Greg was awakened by his daughter asking a simple question: 'Daddy . . . can I come home?'"

Although this isn't a fairy tale with an "and everyone lived happily ever after" ending, one thing is clear—Dr. Greg kept the door open for his daughter to find herself and Christ again. And there's a good chance things are (now) moving in the right direction.

KEITH'S DEFINITION OF FRIENDSHIP

It's time to hear another brother's definition of amity. Keith's seems the most fitting for the story you just experienced: "As iron sharpens iron, so one person sharpens another. (Proverbs 27:17, NASB.)" Every time I think of a true friendship with another man, Proverbs 27:17 pops into my mind. In male relationships, *if* we are being honest/transparent as well as vulnerable, another man can relate and hold you accountable to be the best version of yourself. *If* is the keyword, because in most relationships, especially with men, being transparent and vulnerable is not what we are taught; at least not what *I* was taught.

For most of my life, I did not understand healthy relationships. I thought my personal identity was achieved through others, but those relationships were codependent. There was the constant tension of either manipulating someone for something that I wanted or being manipulated by someone who wanted something from me. In essence, they were purely transactional relationships. But through Jesus, I learned that *He* is my foundation and my identity. When I come from that place, I can be open and vulnerable, which allows others to be open and vulnerable, which leads to true accountability and brotherhood.

CHAPTER 9

Being Successful Just Wasn't Enough for Jake

Dr. Greg's story in the last chapter illustrates why having brothers from a diverse group of professions, histories, and backgrounds is vital to Power of 4's success. Our plurality of thought gave Dr. Greg insight into problems his colleagues and even family members alone couldn't provide. But a man's career is just one type of variety, the story in this chapter deals with another: Age.

Jake came to Power of 4 as our youngest brother. In fact, some men had grandchildren not much younger than Jake's children when he joined us more than a decade ago. His tale shows why it's valuable to have brothers that not only don't come from the same career or industry, but also represent different life stages. After all, our fellowship thrives on different viewpoints, whether driven by career, politics, or any other contributing factor.

Jake has since left Power of 4 to pursue a business opportunity he couldn't pass by. We've stayed on great terms, with regular updates and even an in-person visit from one of our "alumni" earlier in 2022, after COVID-19 restrictions were lifted. Jake gave us permission to use his story, and we've changed names and details as we have throughout this book.

Unlike Dr. Greg's tale, Jake's situation focused on marriage and divorce. But before we get to how it played out for Jake, we must discuss his background, because, like all men, how Jake thinks about relationships was largely shaped by his childhood experiences.

BEING THE YOUNGEST IN A BIG HOUSEHOLD ISN'T EASY

Jake was born into an Irish-Catholic family in the Midwest. He has three brothers and two sisters, but holds a special place in the family as "the baby." His oldest brother is much older, and there's a major age gap between his youngest sibling and him. An unkind observer might call him a "surprise," but luckily for Jake, his parents never said that. Or even hinted it. They favored calling him the family's caboose, or "Tail-End Charlie," World War II slang for the last plane in formation.

In some families, the youngest child is pampered by parents who have learned from their mistakes with older siblings. In Jake's case, being the youngest meant witnessing his mom and dad squabble constantly and being targeted by the older kids for any supposed slight. Jake considers his parents good, hardworking people, but their marriage was strained by his arrival. There were times Jake had to dodge his infuriated father, then an infuriated brother or sister. In his view, his parents' relationship was forever a test of wills. Both wanting to exert power, their struggles often devolved into bitter arguing. He observed that his parents rarely seemed happy together. Instead, they were mostly pleasant *away* from each other.

Although his parents never divorced, plenty of divorce occurred in his family. By the time Jake reached adulthood, several siblings had separated, including a brother who had left his wife by the time Jake graduated high school. These factors combined to give Jake a skewed vision of marriage. It seemed to him that most unions involved a lot of fighting. When the squabbling got too bad, the home would split—whether or not kids were involved. At the same time, growing up in the Roman Catholic church left him confused about religion.

Jake recalls that as a teen he was religiously active in church yet didn't have a clear understanding of what Jesus Christ wanted us to do as Christians. He knew about concepts like grace, but didn't have a clue what they really meant. Church seemed to be heavy on ritual, but light on practical information to lead a better life. In high school, he began distancing himself from his faith. He believed in God, but he didn't dwell on Christianity often. Believing material success to be all that mattered, he moved to California, the land of opportunity.

CATCHING LIGHTNING IN A BOTTLE (OVER AND OVER)

Jake figured out early on he wasn't cut out for a career in a single company—even as the owner. Instead, he found himself in a regular cycle of creating an organization around an innovative product or service, then selling the company as it hit its stride. He called it "catching lightning in a bottle," and had a knack for doing it over and over again. Many years later as this business approach became more common, it was given the name "serial entrepreneurship." (Jake tells us he never uses the term himself—it's too close to serial killer for his liking.)

Still, launching winning startups became his thing, a product of his ingenuity and creativity. Just as soon as he moved to California, Jake spotted business opportunities. His finger on the pulse of the market, he could often see what was coming next, whether it be online or in bricks & mortar retail. Of course, not all his ideas were hits. Anyone who has run their own business knows there are ups and downs. Sometimes the best idea doesn't work out right, sometimes the ROI (return on investment) isn't what it should be. Yet, even with occasional misses, Jake still had a fantastic batting average, plus the worldly goods to prove it.

Despite so much success, Jake felt something lacking. The problem was, for once, he couldn't put his finger on it. Reflecting upon this time with us later, Jake examined his family life. At the time he had loving relationships with his three young children. His marriage was also okay, if slightly distant. In his mind, some detachment was to be expected in a busy life full of long hours making startups work, plus managing busy kids' schedules. Back then Jake did not conclude that a lack of faith was contributing to his growing negativity. Religion had little place in his thoughts. Business was hectic, and the biggest opportunity of all was coming into view: a partnership on a telecom startup with a long-time friend and engineering whiz by the name of Oscar.

A DREAM SHATTERED

Jake and Oscar had collaborated on many startups over the years. They had a reputation for being better at innovating than the heavy hitters in Silicon Valley, which was saying something in the early 2000s when the NorCal tech giants were light years ahead of the pack. Jake and Oscar could think outside of the box, generating elegant solutions to technical problems for less money and time than any bloated organization.

But this time they weren't working on a fix for an in-house

project at Hewlett-Packard or Apple. They were develop-
ing their own innovation they hoped would be a digital
gamechanger. Without going into boring details, Jake had
pinpointed problems limiting telecom providers from adapting their equipment to handle high bandwidth requirements
when streaming came into vogue. He looped in Oscar to
handle technical aspects. Together they dreamed of helping
companies turn their trickle of data into a raging Internet
river. There was just one problem—Jake put too much trust
in Oscar.

As stated, Jake and Oscar had worked together on many
occasions, but never had tackled anything at this scale. Like
our brother Rodney, Jake didn't feel a need to formally protect himself with contracts. He was the very definition of an
innovator flying by the seat of his pants. But as Jake explains,
Oscar cut him out of a deal hatched with a major company to
buy their tech. Worse, Oscar patented the product under his
own name, though it was Jake's idea. In essence, his partner
removed Jake from his own startup, mostly because the other
company wanted 100% ownership of the product and Jake
favored a licensing deal.

Stunned by Oscar's duplicity, Jake vowed to fight back—a
vow that didn't hold up for long. Jake was brought into a
room with his attorney and four lawyers representing the
major company. Their hourly fee combined was more than
Jake paid monthly for his son's tuition, an early warning he
wouldn't have a prayer in court. The high-priced sharks cor-
rectly pointed out that even if he could prove his claims, the
company could keep him tied up in court so long he'd go
bankrupt. They offered him a check for $150,000, meager
compensation for a deal that should have netted him millions. Defeated, Jake took it, wondering if he'd ever make it
back to the big time again.

HOW JAKE JOINED POWER OF 4

After this fiasco, Jake was at a low point. In his early 30s, he felt like he had lost his mojo, the worst thing that can happen to an entrepreneur. The blow to his ego also strained his marriage. You might be thinking, "But he made $150,000!" A reasonable point, but the deal should have paid him much more—millions more. He had placed a lot of his eggs in a single basket. Now he was left with few eggs and no basket. His wife Suzie had also counted on those proverbial chickens hatching.

When Jake stopped feeling sorry for himself and looked around, he found his marriage worse than ever. Financial difficulties were a big culprit. By now he was working on some promising opportunities, but it would be a while before they brought in significant revenue. If at all.

Despite all this, his family still lived extravagantly as they had for years. Buying the latest gadgets and taking lavish vacations put a steady drain on Jake's bank account. Also, the little distance in Jake's marriage had grown. Frequent arguments sparked from the smallest of matters, like a bill for a lawn care service Jake was supposed to have canceled. These petty squabbles escalated at the worst possible times, like when Jake was exhausted from a 12-hour workday and just wanted to sleep.

His deteriorating relationship with his wife Suzie left him depressed, searching for answers. During this time, if Jake wasn't working or watching his children play, he would occasionally go hiking to clear his mind. He knew he wasn't in a good place, professionally or personally. If he didn't change something soon, he was headed for a crash. One day as he climbed a new trail, he did something rash. Getting down on his knees amidst the leaves and dirt, he asked God for help—something he had never done before.

As Jake tells it, he looked heavenward on a beautiful fall day, begging for divine assistance. "God," he said. "I'm sorry I haven't been a good Christian all these years. But I need you now. I need to know what to do with my life. Would my family be better off if I disappeared and never came back? Should I try to get a regular job? Should I stay with my wife? Help me fix myself. Please, Lord."

Praying this way, he didn't expect an immediate answer, but that's what he got. Jake got back on his feet, expecting to find the trail deserted since it wasn't yet 6:00 a.m. Instead, the next instant, he ran into none other than fellow hiker Mark, coming down the hill. Seeing Mark dressed in shorts and a t-shirt surprised Jake. The only other time he had seen Mark he was in a suit and tie at a school fundraiser. As they nibbled on sushi rolls, they had discussed their children, some who played the same sports. They'd also chatted about business a bit, but that was the extent of their conversation.

Still, Jake knew Mark had a reputation as a Christian devoted to his faith without being a Bible-thumper. As Mark approached, Jake said to him, "Mark! I didn't know you were a hiker."

Pleased at the company, the two men spent the next hour enjoying the sun, the breeze, and a little comradery. By the time they were walking to their cars, Jake gathered his courage. He confessed to Mark what he'd been thinking about all morning. "Um, I need some help. Before you got here, I literally asked God for direction. Then you showed up out of nowhere."

"That can't be a coincidence," said Mark with a smile.

Jake was thinking the same thing. "I'd like to reconnect with my faith. Is that something you could help me with?"

Looking back, Mark admires Jake for being so vulnerable. He didn't know Mark well and could have been met with mockery or disparagement. As he says, "Jake took a leap of faith we've all taken in our own way. I knew just what he needed because I'd been there before."

That day at the foot of the hill, Mark gave Jake three immediate suggestions. The first was to read *The Purpose Driven Life* by Pastor Rick Warren. The second was to join him at church on Sunday. And the third? Join Power of 4, of course.

Jake took all of Mark's advice with great gusto. He devoured the book. He joined Mark's family at church, even bringing two of his own children, and he joined Power of 4 at our next meeting. You could tell right away the meetings were nourishment for Jake's hungry soul. Here was a man who didn't have strong relationships with other men and hadn't for years. He needed brothers with whom he could discuss his problems and receive non-judgmental advice without the fear of betrayal. Jake's openness was especially poignant because he never felt close to his older brothers or even his dad, previously his strongest male influences.

Even so, not everything was going as smoothly as Jake hoped.

A MARRIAGE FRACTURED BY FAITH?

With Power of 4's support Jake made real strides. Faith in Jesus helped him feel like a new person. His depression lifted, and he was working on commercial ideas with renewed passion. Money was still tight because so many projects were stuck in the pre-launch phase, but he was feeling better and actively participating in every Power of 4 meeting. Just one problem remained. One that frankly surprised us: Suzie was not onboard with his renewed interest in Christianity.

In fact, his wife seemed outright resentful of his faith, not to mention his interest in Power of 4. Her displeasure incited fresh arguments. One time the family was eating dinner in front of the TV when the news mentioned abortion. Jake announced he was now pro-life. His wife stared daggers at him before yelling, "You used to be pro-choice. You start attending a church and suddenly you're some right-winger!"

Jake stayed calm, explaining to her, "This isn't about church. It's about a baby having a heartbeat in the womb. I was pro-choice, but that's only because I never thought about this stuff deeply before." To his happy surprise, Jake's kids nodded in agreement with his commonsense explanation. This only made Suzie madder. For the next few weeks, she used Jake's new faith to needle him. After he got into a minor car accident, she asked him why Jesus didn't come down from Heaven to stop it. Jake did his best to roll with the punches, but nothing could prepare him for what was yet to come.

POWER OF 4 FIGHTS
TO SAVE A MARRIAGE

We were gathered for our typical Sunday meeting at a diner off the 405 freeway when Jake, looking drained, asked to speak. Anytime a brother makes this request, you know something is up. Still, what we heard surprised all of us.

Out of nowhere, Jake's wife had given him an ultimatum. She told him to move into the family's beach house so she could have her space. Of course, they had had their problems and arguments for years, especially lately, but there was no obvious tipping point that led to this demand. Jake told us that he had moved out at her request and kept himself busy with work, but needed advice as badly as he did the day he met Mark on the hike.

Nick began the discussion. "Now I'm no math whiz, but it seems like this happened days ago since you had time to move. Why're we all sitting here in shock over the news on *Sunday*? Why didn't you reach out to us earlier?"

Jake shrugged. "You've all explained that it's important to inform everyone of a major crisis, but I didn't want to make waves as the new guy. I didn't want you all to think I'm complicating stuff for you."

Around the table we all shook our heads. Nick softened his tone. "You don't need to worry about our feelings. We talk about 'coming ugly,' and that means being transparent, warts and all. We've talked about your marriage before, and none of your brothers here will judge you for your problems—even if this had been your very first meeting."

Mark concurred. "Nick's right. We can't help you unless we know about a serious problem as soon as possible. We've dealt with practically every relationship mess there can be, and we'll help you through this. Now, what do you think led Suzie to ask you to leave?"

Jake reflected on the past few weeks. "She's feeling confused, angry, directionless. Like how I felt a few months ago. I think she's blaming everything on me, but our family life wasn't bad before, and our financials have always been up and down—it's part of the game when you're starting new companies."

Nick focused on a topic that he had in common with Jake: young kids at home. "You've been away for a few days, how are your children taking it?"

"They seem to be holding up. I have a strong relationship with each, and I told them this isn't their fault, that we'll work it out. I've also seen them every day since moving, even if just to grab a snack before practice."

Steve had purposefully waited to go last. He asked a simple question: "You're known for your business vision. I'm sure you've thought about how this will play out. What do you expect will happen over the next year or so?"

Steve was right. Jake had thought ahead. "Well, I expect we'll get lawyers soon, then paperwork gets filed. We'll have some hearings and start valuing property, talking about custody. I don't know how long all this takes, frankly."

Though Jake was being stoic, Steve could sense his profound hurt. "I understand why you see things going this way, but you shouldn't write off your marriage so soon. Jesus believes a marriage is worth fighting to preserve. In my own life, I've worked with many people whose marriages were in crisis, some in much worse shape than yours—and they came back from the brink." Steve turned to the group. "What do you think? Should Jake try to fix his marriage?"

We all nodded.

Mark spoke next. He told Jake, "When we met on the hill that day, you were brave enough to ask for my help. You've already come a long way by embracing your faith and turning to your new brothers for advice. I think Steve's right—you *do* have another chance to make a journey towards positivity, but this time it must be with your wife. Not on your own. Are you ready for that challenge?"

Almost immediately, Jake felt his spirits lift. "I hadn't thought about the possibility of reconciliation. Maybe I was just in shock. Things seemed so final, but I don't want them to be. How can I start to repair things?"

Each brother provided Jake with suggestions. Nick advised writing a letter to Suzie expressing his true feelings. Steve recommended keeping attention on the kids, finding common ground over their shared wish to give them a good life. Mark emphasized Jake's need to remain strong in his faith. Turning to Jesus had changed Jake's life, and the Lord would continue helping him through this crisis. Last, he suggested that after reestablishing communication, Jake should ask

Suzie to attend counseling together—whether in a Christian setting or a non-religious one.

LIGHT AT THE END OF THE TUNNEL?

Jake left that meeting feeling energized. Just a few hours before, he had resigned himself to divorce and a protracted custody battle. Now, the first steps of a plan rolled around in his brain, just like one of his many business ideas. His mission was straightforward—to reestablish communication with his wife and fix their marriage together as a team.

Over the coming months, Power of 4 received regular updates from Jake. We always heard from him at length in our sessions, but we also got group texts or emails when something important happened. One thing was clear to all of us from the start—Jake wished to stay with his wife. Wanting to figure out a solution to their problems, he threw his energy into it full force.

Suzie responded favorably to Jake's outreach. After receiving his letter, she called him and they had a long heart-to-heart, the sort that often doesn't happen in a marriage when both spouses are so busy working and raising kids. Their deep talks continued. Soon after, Suzie agreed to meet for dinner at a restaurant special to them. Suzie pointed out that they hadn't dined there alone in three years, although it was where they celebrated her first pregnancy years ago.

Jake calmly admitted that she was right. He also took responsibility for not paying more attention to her. "It's no excuse, but I thought I was doing my part by focusing on the business—bringing in the money."

Suzie, in turn, apologized for picking fights when Jake was vulnerable. "I hit below the belt. That wasn't right," she said, taking his hand in hers.

This wasn't the only positive that came out of that dinner. As Steve suggested, Jake brought up marriage counseling over wine. Suzie flatly refused a Christian counselor but was open to seeing a non-religious one. Seizing the opportunity, Jake worked to find a counselor the very next day. Based on Steve's advice, Jake was careful to include Suzie in the decision-making. She felt invested and approached their sessions with the same level of energy.

Counseling proved revealing for both parties. Jake learned Suzie felt he had replaced her with his faith, his church, and most of all, his new men's group. This floored Jake. *How could the most important person in his life feel replaced?* He also discovered financial insecurity was a major concern for Suzie, who had turned to pills to fight the anxiety gnawing at her mind. In the counselor's opinion, their marriage *was* solid in terms of their love for each other, but they had to communicate better.

The sessions helped them open up in ways they hadn't in years. It was clear to all involved that they were on the road to reconciliation. After months of good developments, Jake moved back home, much to the joy of his children. The marriage has done well in the years since. Suzie has not only embraced Jake's faith but has since joined him in church. The family relocated to NorCal soon after the reconciliation, and although they are in a new setting, their restored marriage remains strong due to open communication lines.

HOW POWER OF 4 HELPED JAKE

Jake tells us he gives our group much credit for saving his marriage. He explains, "Most men I knew socially back then were in their early 30s like me. Even if I was willing to 'come ugly' with them, they'd have similar perspectives. Because Power of 4 offers diverse outlooks from men at various ages and from different walks of life, I could see my situation from different vantage points."

Also, the non-judgmental way Power of 4 works together was critical. This young man is a problem solver. He makes things work and doesn't fail often. Like his last business endeavor, he felt like his marriage was a disappointment. This was hard to admit. Despite that feeling, Jake had confidence that his brothers in Christ would treat him with respect. Also, problem solvers like Jake often struggle when challenges hit too close to home. They can't see the forest for the trees. Jake therefore thrived on getting advice from people *outside* of his situation possessing relevant life experiences.

Thinking back to that first meeting after Suzie asked him to leave, Jake says, "Some things the group told me weren't surprises. I knew I was going to the right people for advice. I felt paralyzed, but I also knew Power of 4 could get me moving. What I didn't anticipate was that these men, whom I proudly call brothers, would stand up for my marriage and advise me throughout to not give up. They never gave up and said, 'Call a lawyer,' because they recognized what our counselor (and later my wife and I) recognized: Our marriage had everything it needed to work if we just communicated better."

Jake says without hesitation that restoring his faith in Jesus Christ was the ultimate moment for him, and he's thankful to Power of 4 for supporting and encouraging him in this regard. Those are big sentiments, and Power of 4 takes pride in his success and his friendship.

JAKE'S DEFINITION OF FRIENDSHIP

Jake credits much of his current success in NorCal to the sagacious advice he's received from his Power of 4 brothers over the years. Below is his definition of friendship:

Of the many people who we meet throughout our lives, we tend to categorize them using a pretty simple system. We label them friends, acquaintances, colleagues, and sometimes enemies. But what I've learned later in life is that true friends are rarer (and more valuable) than gold. True friends are the men who will stop what they are doing to help you even when there is nothing in it for them. They are the people that I would do anything for (that doesn't violate my faith) without a second thought.

I once believed that this type of friendship was usually found in the movies or the war novels I enjoy reading on the beach. But then I joined Power of 4, and saw this type of friendship, best described by the term brotherhood, in action every week.

CHAPTER 10

Wade's Temptation and a Lifestyle Left Behind

Many challenges Power of 4 brothers bring to the group involve sins. That shouldn't surprise anyone. As we've documented, we are all sinners. We are fallen thanks to Adam and Eve. As Christians, we work daily to overcome our sins and hopefully not repeat them. But sin is tricky. Sins of the past don't always stay in the rear-view mirror. Sometimes they return to tempt us again. Anyone who has worked to overcome an addiction to drugs, alcohol, porn—or countless other negative things—can attest to the fact that vigilance is required.

Then again, some people fortunate enough to never have experienced an addiction think disentanglement is as easy as saying, "Just stop the behavior." It never is. Just like losing weight isn't as simple as saying, "Eat less," there are many factors at play here, including psychological and emotional elements. Add to that mix the poison of sinful behavior—or the temptation of returning to a sinful way of life—and you have yourself a major struggle.

Our brother Wade went through just such a challenge with the help of Power of 4. He has since relocated to New Mexico where he started his own group. His tale, shared with names and details changed, is a story of addiction not to a particular drug, but to a *lifestyle*—one he thought he left behind.

Instead, it unexpectedly reappeared, luring him right back.

KILLING IT IN COMPUTER LAND

Like many of our brothers, Wade came up in tech. He joined the computer industry in the '80s and was instantly a sales machine. He had the knowledge to converse with programmers, yet also the people skills to rub elbows with executives who hardly knew what a hard drive was. Back then there wasn't yet a computer on every desk. Laptops were lumbering heavy contraptions no one wished to carry around, and smartphones were but the stuff of science fiction.

Wade's ability to bridge the gap between wielding computer know-how and navigating corporate America quickly distinguished him amongst his peers. Now, in any vertical a continuum of importance and responsibility exists. In the computer sales world at that time, at one end were the lowly store clerks who helped retail customers buy an Apple or PC computer. At the other were professionals like Wade who hobnobbed with suits at large outfits rolling out thousands of workstations—and their supporting networks and servers. As a CEO of a mid-size company once told Wade, "I trust you more than my own COO. You ever want a job outside of sales, give me a ring."

In time, Wade became an industry tastemaker, influencing the market as to what was up-and-coming. And, although he worked for a big distributor instead of his own business, he was a star salesman making insane money. Possessing the trust of his bigwig clients, he shaped how others in the field approached their jobs. Whenever Wade suggested a particular computer brand or accessory product to his customers, many coworkers followed suit.

As the computer industry continued booming into the early '90s, manufacturers took note of guys like Wade. It turned out, getting key sales executives to push their product was just as important as flashy packaging or hitting a particular price point. All seemed well. But a new era in Wade's life was quietly forming, one that would involve a dark lifestyle.

RISE OF THE SILICON COWBOYS

A major market shift occurred at this time. Once seen as specialized tools, computers were becoming vital necessities for every white-collar worker. Meanwhile, home computing took off like a rocket. Not long ago, computer advertising mostly appeared in trade magazines. Now they were in Super Bowl ads, featured in commercials like Intel's dancing "spacemen." Also, brands outside of Apple were becoming household names. Money poured into courting sales execs like Wade, powerful individuals who could make or break a product just by introducing it to their corporate customers.

Aware of this reality, savvy manufacturers began peddling their wares to Wade and other impresarios of his caliber. They used techniques you may be familiar with from medical sales, whereby doctors receive perks, like paid-for cruises, to learn about a new treatment in some lovely tropical paradise. For Wade, the door officially opened when an up-and-coming computer syndicate invited him to a private function at the annual Consumer Electronics Show (CES). Held in "Sin City" Las Vegas, CES is *the* stage for companies to unveil cutting-edge tech. For Wade, it became his entry point to the good life. Or at least what he *thought* was the good life.

That first CES party had it all. Dancing strippers, free alcohol by the gallon, designer drugs. An extrovert who loved mingling, he was easily hooked. He spent a sleepless weekend living it up thanks to an endless supply of cocaine. Coke helped him bond with other sales execs from around the country. They gave themselves the name "The Silicon Cowboys" and promised to keep in touch. (That moniker may seem hopelessly quaint these days, but remember: This was back when computers offered the latest gold rush, and Silicon Valley was just entering the lexicon as both a place and a cultural touchstone.)

Wade's star was ascending with no sign of stopping. The partying climbed with it. In no time, the Silicon Cowboys began demanding more from their private soirées than dancing strippers. High-end call girls replaced them, along with variety in the drugs department. The Silicon Cowboys saw themselves as rock stars and insisted on the same hedonistic lifestyle.

The parties became ever more frequent and more outrageous. Often organized on short notice, they soon featured drugs like "ecstasy" and "special K" that were making the rounds in exclusive nightclubs. Wade can (barely) recall a trip to NorCal to celebrate the launch of new software. It stands out as little more than brief flashes of faces, flesh, and music. A concerned Silicon Cowboy later told him, "It's a miracle you weren't arrested in Palo Alto." To this day Wade doesn't know what he meant—which makes it worse.

Wade's hard partying shifted from something intermittent—something that only occurred during special trips—to being his regular weekend plans. He drank and snorted coke most weekends while going through an endless parade of women, mostly one-night stands. Looking back, he admits he can't remember what many looked like, let alone their names. He says he was never addicted to drinking or cocaine, along with drugs like Valium that smoothed out the high, but he was a heavy and habitual user.

Yet even with all the debauchery, he was somehow always

put together for the work week, where his high-power clients required him to be sharp. If any ever detected his Monday morning hangover, they never mentioned it. The Silicon Cowboys roamed far and wide, cavorting their way through the '90s. These were wildly successful young men making obscene cash and partying like there was no tomorrow. Although Wade enjoyed the giant bank account, the beautiful women, and the VIP parties, he began questioning things.

Despite it all, he knew something was missing in his life. That's when he went to his closest friend in the gang, an East Coast sales rep named Mitchell.

One night Wade asked him if he felt the same. "Mitch, I sure never thought selling computers would lead to having a girl in each arm in the hottest club in all of Vegas but . . .. Don't you ever feel like there has to be more to life?"

Mitchell looked at Wade like he just sprouted a second head. "You crazy? We're living the dream. We can't slow down. Not now."

"Yeah, but—"

"'Anything more than this, the hottest club in Vegas?' What more do you want?"

"I don't know."

Mitchell punched him in the arm. "I'd hate to find out you're going soft."

Punching him back, Wade assured his friend there was nothing wrong. But a seed had planted in the back of his mind. If the Silicon Cowboy lifestyle wasn't fulfilling him the way it did Mitchell and the others, did he need to make a change? After a minute or so of musing, he drowned out further thoughts with a bottle of champagne that cost more than most people's monthly mortgage.

Nevertheless, that seed was planted. And soon it would grow.

FINDING CHRIST AND
HANGING UP THE SPURS

It didn't happen like in the movies.

There was no cataclysmic event that turned Wade from his sinful ways. Instead, doubt about his lifestyle grew and grew. He became more aware of how his decisions were harming him. He also worried about the health effects of sustained drug and alcohol abuse, even if he didn't consider himself an addict. AIDS was in the cultural zeitgeist, and he fretted over contracting it and other sexually transmitted diseases. He also began to see the glory days of industry parties fading as the playing field leveled. He no longer had the same star power he once enjoyed because no one really did—luminary status was now reserved for CEOs like Apple's Steve Jobs.

All valid concerns, for sure, yet there was one deeper reason Wade knew it was time for a change. Over time he had become aware that there was a gaping hole in the center of his being. No amount of wine, women, or partying filled it. Even his gargantuan paydays held less appeal.

During his last trip to Vegas, it was abundantly clear Sin City didn't cut it any longer. Like so many men who came to flourish in Power of 4, Wade realized the hole he perceived was caused by a turning away from God. Wade believed in Jesus, but he hadn't attended church in years, didn't regularly pray, and hardly thought about the Lord.

All of this changed when Wade met the right woman.

TURNING OVER A NEW LEAF

Stephanie was a stunner. Some friends—not the Silicon Cowboys variety—set them up on a blind date. Wade and Stephanie clicked from the start, leaving him marveling that of all the women he had gone through, he had never met one as pretty as Stephanie, nor as intelligent. Equally attracted to Wade, Stephanie surprised him by telling him he had a reputation as a party boy, something she wasn't interested in pursuing.

Until then, Wade had never stopped to think what others thought about his lifestyle. It just never occurred to him that the woman of his dreams might be put off by his past. Party girls never seemed to mind his rep. They were along for the ride.

But Stephanie was *different*. She set ground rules for Wade. If he ever hoped to be with her, he had to clean up his act. His habit of drinking to excess had to go. Same with his casual drug use. And one more thing: He had to be 100% monogamous. No more carousing. Those days were done. Disenchanted with the life he led; Wade readily agreed to all these conditions. Then he did one better. He asked Stephanie to attend church with her. It wasn't long before he received his second baptism and became a practicing Christian.

Wade and Stephanie's relationship grew more serious as he shed his former lifestyle. He stopped going to parties and dropped old friends like Mitchell. Amazed by Wade's commitment to change, Stephanie fell deeper in love by the day. But these changes had repercussions on Wade's career, not just his relationship.

Still a top sales performer, Wade's transformation hurt him professionally. It distanced him from his former revelers, the movers and shakers who commanded powerful industry influence. Naturally, the Silicon Cowboys didn't like seeing one of their own drop out. They would never admit it, but his choosing Christ and a *woman* over them served as a reprimand. It reminded them of their own sin—even if they would never use this term.

Meanwhile, the corporate partners who organized so many raucous events didn't like his abstention either. Almost immediately, they excluded him from party invites. They also kept him out of the loop on product information and professional networking. For the first time, he had to go through official channels to get demo products or pre-launch details, instead of having manufacturers knocking on his door bearing gifts.

Despite job concerns, every other area of Wade's life was right on track. Engaged, he hadn't touched cocaine in months, and rarely drank alcohol. He was feeling great about his relationship not only with his soon-to-be-wife, but also with the Lord. The distance from his old pals hurt somewhat, but he liked his new path. He also had the wisdom to see seismic changes occurring in the industry. In a prescient move, he made the call he had been thinking about since Stephanie accepted his proposal.

ONE DOOR CLOSES. ANOTHER OPENS

That important call was to the CEO who offered him a job years before. Our Silicon Cowboy was now officially hanging up his spurs, taking a corporate job as a senior IT executive of a large corporation. It was a testament to Wade's abilities that he managed this career transition so smoothly. Even more impressive, he pulled it off while going straight and getting married. His transition to "Wade 2.0," was complete upon starting his new executive role.

The funny thing about beginning a new job is that most people you now work with don't know much about you. This was the case for Wade. He presented himself as a clean-living Christian guy. Therefore, his coworkers assumed that's the way he'd always been. He can recall two subordinates discussing a TV show once. One said to the other, "The main character did a 'key bump' right in the car. He was undercover and had to convince the drug dealer he wasn't a cop." Then he turned to Wade to explain, "A 'key bump' is when you scoop up cocaine using a key and snort it right off the metal."

Wade suppressed a smile as he replied, "Oh, thanks, I was wondering about that. Hope the cop drove off safely!" Of course, his well-meaning coworkers had no clue Wade had done plenty of key bumps in his party days. Not only that, but he had also seen many an old friend snort cocaine off of practically anything else you can think off, including a woman's body.

Wade's life ran smoothly in this manner for years. He and Stephanie had children and settled into a faith-centered life of positivity, including several career advancements that kept their suburban lives comfortable. Around this time, Wade joined Power of 4 at the suggestion of Andrew.

A member of the same church Wade attended; Andrew knew a bit about Wade's past. Andrew had a feeling that when Wade made his life change, he also removed himself from any male network. Yes, the support from the old group wasn't positive, but it was still support. Absent such ties, Wade needed the right group to kept him on the path. It so happens, Power of 4 was also seeking a new brother at this time.

Wade's life was running on all cylinders, but he was about to face old temptations. They arrived in a completely unexpected manner.

SHOCKING NEWS AT A WEDDING

Although most of the Silicon Cowboys excluded Wade after he turned his life towards Christianity, he remained in touch with a few of the guys. He was pleased to receive a wedding invitation from a former compatriot who now lived in Seattle and worked for Microsoft. Like Wade, he too, had cleaned himself up and left the party scene years ago. Wade was eager to attend the ceremony and see old friends, never dreaming of the danger awaiting him. But first, Wade enjoyed the wedding.

As he introduced Stephanie to buddies he hadn't seen in years, he reminisced (in a "PG" way) about their past. Conversing along, he kept looking for one person, his old pal Mitchell. Wade hadn't talked with Mitchell for years, mostly because the latter never approved of his Christian faith or his marriage. Last Wade had heard, he was still a partyer cutting loose every weekend, even as he continued to climb the corporate ladder.

Finally, Wade couldn't take it anymore. He asked a group of friends, "Where's Mitchell? I've been looking all over for him."

The five men exchanged glances. At last, one of them said "No one told you?"

Wade was confused. "Told me what?"

"Mitchell killed himself last year. He was diagnosed with a heart problem and decided to eat a bullet instead of slowing down."

Wade was crushed.

His old friend was dead, and no one had bothered to tell him. This shock caused a ripple effect in his life. He wasn't tempted to suddenly return to the lifestyle that killed Mitchell, but he did feel the need to take better care of himself. In the last decade, his metabolism had slowed, like so many men, and he packed on the pounds. He couldn't shake the image of himself in a doctor's office getting a similar diagnosis.

Who knew what damage all the partying could have done to him in his younger years?

Of course, he talked about this incident with Power of 4. We advised him to rationally confront his fears. He had stopped abusing his body long before Mitchell's diagnosis and was in good health. Still, we suggested he begin to exercise more and carefully watch his food intake. Wade was game. An initiator by nature, he flew into action with a new health regimen. We could sense he intended to erase his fears by sweating them out.

So far so good. We didn't know what would happen next.

TEMPTATION

Wade joined a fitness club popular with professionals in The OC, tweaking his schedule so he could hit the gym daily before coming into the office. He approached fitness with his usual zeal, initially working out with a personal trainer, then managing a fitness program on his own. He was slowly seeing results, losing flab, and toning his muscles. He enjoyed how his gym sessions made him feel good, enabling him to stay sharper later in the day.

He also noticed something else as he lifted weights and ran on the treadmill—a gorgeous girl leading aerobics class in a glass-walled room beside him. It didn't take long for Wade to grow obsessed with the young woman. He didn't know her name, but he found himself thinking about her all the time.

He's not proud to admit it now, but he even rearranged his days so he could watch her more as she led classes with inexhaustible energy. He began tracking her different outfits, primarily skintight and skimpy. He fantasized about signing up for her class, then asking her out for lunch. It got so bad that he caught himself daydreaming in work meetings about running off to Vegas with her for a lost weekend of sex and cocaine. Basically, his thoughts had turned dark, and he was feeling temptation to pursue her.

He knew he needed help, and he knew where to find it.

HOW WE HELPED WADE

As discussed, transparency is a critical component to Power of 4. Because brothers come ugly, we knew the background on Wade's party days. We also knew about the shock of Mitchell's death and how it influenced Wade to make healthy choices his new "North Star." When we come ugly, our brothers need less background to understand a man's problem. To his credit—and his benefit—Wade's candor helped us swing into action as soon as we learned of the fitness instructor's tractor beam pull on him.

Over a few sessions, Wade explained the situation and his dark thoughts, then asked for feedback. As we always do, we went around the table asking questions in a non-judgmental way. Steve started us off. He wanted to know how far this temptation had gone. "Wade, just to be clear. You haven't had any direct contact with this woman at all, right?"

"No, thank God." Wade answered. Then he added, "I haven't talked to her. Not even once. I also haven't talked to anyone at the fitness club *about* her. I don't even know her name." He said this last part sheepishly.

"Look, you don't need to be embarrassed here, Wade," said Mark. "It sounds like this is mostly an infatuation with your mental fantasy of the woman. Any guy with a pulse might be tempted like this."

Andrew picked up on this theme. "Wade, what is it about her that has you head over heels?"

Wade grinned. "What can I say? She's hot."

Steve held up a finger. "Don't try to downplay things. *Come uglier.* What about her attracts you so much?"

Wade's body language revealed he was holding something back. "You guys haven't seen her. She wears provocative outfits that aren't much more than a bikini. You guys get it."

Steve nodded, remaining non-judgmental. "Thanks for being honest. It isn't comfortable to say this stuff aloud, but that's why we call it 'coming ugly.' All of us have had sexual thoughts about a woman at one time or another. We're men, and we're fallen beings. When a woman has a body like that, we can't always help things, can we?"

Before Wade could answer, Mark changed the topic. "Wade, we've been talking about the gym bunny, but how are things with Stephanie? Is your marriage suffering?"

Wade confidently replied, "Not at all. We're strong, actually. She's happy I've been getting in shape, and our love life is better than it's been in years. She doesn't know a thing about the fitness club situation, of course."

Andrew switched things back to the mystery woman. "Wade, given everything you know from your past and the new life you've forged, would you really *want* to escalate things with this woman?"

Wade sighed. "You know I wouldn't. That's why I'm sitting here. I left my life of chasing girls in the dust decades ago, and in my heart, I know trying to run off with some instructor would leave me feeling just as empty as I felt before Stephanie. The problem is, I can't help but be attracted to her, and that impacts my thinking even after I leave the club. It's making me a bit crazy."

Steve spoke again after the others. "So, we have a situation where you are tempted by a woman—almost to the point of insanity," he said half-kidding. "Still, you haven't acted on it.

You also know it's not something you want to do, despite the gym bunny's allure. Would you agree the primary challenge here is putting an end to this temptation?"

Wade had to think about that. "Yeah, absolutely. I have a good wife and family already. I'm not interested in throwing that all away, but when I'm in the zone and I see her body moving, I feel powerless to resist. But what can I do? Request they hire unattractive aerobics instructors?"

We chuckled, but it was Mark who answered. "You just gave yourself your answer. You can't remove her from the situation, but you can remove *yourself*. My advice is to switch to one of the many other fitness clubs nearby. Find one that gives you a less distracting view as you work up a sweat."

The other brothers concurred. The situation was not likely to improve if Wade continued to see the exercise instructor daily. In fact, it could worsen if Wade wasn't careful. One way to remove her from his thoughts was to remove her from his senses—a goal easily accomplished by relocating. Furthermore, the group suggested Wade needn't talk to Stephanie about the temptation. Despite her beauty, any woman would suffer a self-confidence hit if her husband admitted lusting after someone 20 years her junior. Also, Wade hadn't acted on the temptation in any significant way, and their marriage was otherwise in great shape.

Wade took our suggestions to heart. He joined one of the gyms Power of 4 suggested and found it a much better environment. Without the aerobics instructor unwittingly tempting him, he returned to normal. The next Power of 4 meeting Wade reported his success to the group. At the second meeting after, he even looked surprised when one of us broached the subject.

"Holy cow! I just realized: I haven't thought about her all week."

That was the last time we talked of Wade's temptation in a group setting.

THE LESSONS WADE TOOK FROM COMING UGLY

As the above makes clear, Wade needed someone to talk to. The temptation he faced was not something he could discuss at home or with strangers. He required a particular setting, an environment filled with fellow men he could trust and who had similar life experiences. Power of 4 supplied all that. We shed light on his situation, helping him to see it in another way.

There was one more benefit. Most importantly to helping Wade—Power of 4 remained non-judgmental throughout the process. A supportive group must never make value statements as a brother tries to do the right thing. It's counterproductive to call a man weak-willed, or even to ask, "What's wrong with you?"

Still, being non-judgmental *does not* mean agreeing that a particular behavior is okay. And it certainly *does not* prevent brothers from probing when they feel the group is not getting the full truth. One critical lesson for Wade was the (continuing) need for transparency. Because he was so candid about his present situation and the past, we could provide him the best advice. This came about because we knew so much about his life. A central facet of transparency is coming ugly—confessing sins. By opening up about his lustful thoughts, we understood the nature of the situation—and fast. Also, other brothers came ugly themselves, admitting that they had battled lustful thoughts. This admission eased Wade's mind. It was easier to deal with the situation surrounded by men who had walked a mile in the same shoes.

Through this experience, Wade learned the true Power of 4. It wasn't just support or brotherhood—it was diverse viewpoints and life experiences that showed him new ways to think about his problem. When men are in crisis, we often can't see the big picture. We get hung up on trivial details, which can lead to bad decisions. Wade is a smart guy. If he wasn't in the thick of the situation, he would have realized that simply changing fitness centers was his best bet.

Power of 4, with the advantage of an outside perspective, immediately zeroed in on a solution that would help put temptation behind him. As Wade explains, "I put all my cards on the table, knowing that the men around me were friends and brothers that wanted to help me stay true to myself, my marriage, my family, and my Christian faith. I trusted them, and they came through with a plan of action. I never felt so supported in my life, and that's why I started a group in my new hometown as soon as I settled in."

WADE'S DEFINITION OF FRIENDSHIP

Andrew invited Wade to join Power of 4 because he saw that a man like him—one who recently upended his life, accepting Jesus Christ as his Lord and Savior—needed support of like-minded men. Power of 4 represents the polar opposite way of being from that of Wade's past. This makes it the ideal group for helping him move forward. Wade described his definition of friendship this way:

As I assess my relationships with friends through the years, I find myself using the term "best friends" with a sense of protection and confidence. I have a handful of best friends that I can count on without a thought of hesitancy. They are the ones that know me best and have been there through my challenges and joys. They give me a sense of security that reminds me that, as I deal with different relationships, I can table some conversations until I'm with my best and closest friends. I always desired to come to gatherings with a group of guys without my guard up, feeling relaxed, feeling like I could share whatever I wanted to share, and anticipate both their responses and them sharing their journeys with me. Power of 4 has provided that for me, and I am extremely thankful for each of my brothers!

PART

HOW TO MAKE THIS HAPPEN

What follows are tips to fine-tune your Power of 4 brotherhood as well as FAQs (frequently asked questions) to set you up for success. Our final chapter contains anonymous feedback from brothers' family members, recounting its influence upon the men in their lives.

CHAPTER 11

Best Practices to Form Your Group Today

Now that you have learned about the reasons men need Power of 4 and experienced stories of some of the brothers (both past and present) describing the value it brings, let's shift our focus to the practical. In the first of two instructional chapters, we will offer best practices, investigating various topics of importance.

HOW TO BEGIN

For starters, don't call it an "accountability group" when courting prospects. This is not the way to build trust. And as we know, trust is critical. Likewise, don't begin with the idea of checking off prospects' challenges. Here's the wrong way to do it: "Prospective brother, do you look at porn or drink too much? Are you tempted to stray from your marriage?" An approach like that is off-putting. It also erroneously suggests we are an accountability group focused on solutions you might find at an AA meeting. It's bound to scare off men you may want to join your Power of 4.

Next, we suggest you turn to prayer when starting out. Lay some names of men on your heart that you think could benefit from the group—and could help others in their own journeys. Once you have your list, don't hesitate. Act now. Tell the candidates you're putting together a group to work through life issues in a safe environment. Tell them you intend to discuss all the bumps, bruises, etc. we all have encountered and continue to face.

In your ask, we also recommend distinguishing between the following:

* Accountability Groups

* Mastermind Groups

* Bible Study Groups

This will show them how Power of 4 differs from all the others.

CHOOSING A LOCATION

We recommend selecting places that are comfortable and offer privacy. A restaurant counts so long as it offers the above. Someone's office can also be good. If you opt for the former, we recommend selecting a booth or table away from others. If it's in an office, we suggest hosting meetings during off-times (e.g., the weekends) so you won't be disturbed.

We first met at Steve's office for the intimacy aspect, knowing that we weren't likely to be interrupted. Another consideration: Introverts are likely to be reticent in public settings. If you choose a public venue, it may lower their comfort level, reducing intimacy and trust, essential to the process. Note: Houses can solve these considerations so long as you're afforded privacy.

FREQUENCY

We like to meet twice a month. There are groups that meet weekly. We find that's too much. 24 times a year is the right amount for us. Then again, some people meet monthly. But there's a danger to not meeting quite so often. Imagine one of your brothers travels a lot for business. If you only meet once a month and he misses that session, it will be two months before he gets to meet with you again. This man is likely to feel like he's not a full brother. Similarly, his brothers miss out in this scenario too. They're equally harmed by not getting to meet with the full group and all the benefits it affords.

MEETING VIRTUALLY VS. IN-PERSON

Teleconferencing via Zoom or Microsoft Teams can be a substitute for IRL (in real life) encounters, but not nearly as good. Of course, we met via remote sessions during the COVID-19 pandemic, but it wasn't ideal. One of the principles reinforcing this is the so-called "7% Rule." It comes from research performed in the 1960s by Professor Albert Mehrabian and his colleagues at UCLA. According to their findings, out of a score of 100% (representing a person's entire interpretation of what someone else said), total communication breaks down into these revealing percentages.

* 7% The weight of the actual words being spoken.

* 38% The tone with which the words are expressed.

* 55% The body language of the speaker.

As you can see, more than *half* of communication in a typical interaction relies on nonverbal behavior. On Zoom you miss out on so much of the cues enabling you to interpret someone's thoughts and emotions. Of course, meeting in person isn't always perfect either. You can be physically present but mentally checked out. (Especially if you're on your phone.) Don't do this.

Moreover, meeting in person has another benefit beyond the richness of sensory details. It shows your sacrifice to be there. It demonstrates your investment in the others. There is an energy to meeting in person. You are anticipating being with others in the moment. A live concert offers a helpful corollary. Seeing your favorite band in person is a vastly different experience than listening to a song on Spotify.

Zoom and other teleconferencing apps also tend to make us into observers rather than being present. For one thing, the nature of the technology allows you to focus more on how *you* look than the people around you. It also prevents deep connection. There is no fist-bumping, handshaking, or hugging online.

Of course, there will be times when teleconferencing is an attractive option—even if it's not the best. Steve recently moved to Texas, but all our other brothers still reside in SoCal. We don't want to miss being with him so for now all of us meet in person—usually at a diner or restaurant—but bring Steve in via Zoom as a work-around.

TIME COMMITMENT

We generally meet for 1.5-2 hours each session. Because we get together biweekly, we need this amount of time to sufficiently address and process everything. Conversely, the first group Steve was in met for one hour. They accomplished their meetings well but only because of the tight structure. There was no friendly chatter in Steve's one-hour meetings. Due to time constraints, they got right to business. Since then, Steve has come to advocate for a more relaxed model encouraging deepness over hard and fast time limits.

Frequency of meetings can affect duration. If you only meet monthly, we recommend a minimum of two hours per session. One more time consideration: our group tends to meet at different restaurants each time to honor the distance men must drive. (We balance it out so brothers can share the driving burden amongst each other.)

DIVERSITY OF OCCUPATIONS, WEALTH, AND CIRCUMSTANCES

There's much benefit to receiving other points of view. Sharing your thoughts with a group possessing myriad life experiences is immensely helpful. Disparate viewpoints are a good thing. Not only does this avoid groupthink dangers, but it also affords the brothers with a plurality of thoughts and ideas.

Along these lines, conferring with individuals outside your occupation is likely to bring you insights you might not otherwise receive. Professionals in different industries are bound to see things differently. This goes even for brothers who have retired. They too, will have a different and unique life experience, affecting how they interpret situations.

Steve knows this well. He has been in groups with 20-, 30-, 40-, and 60-year-olds, and appreciates the diversity of opinions he received due to their makeup. Here's one example: A younger man may not possess the same business wisdom as a man with several decades on him. Likewise, an older brother can benefit from the fresh perspective of a young pup just starting out.

Even so, we offer this advice with a caveat. If your prospects view brotherhood as a networking opportunity to enhance their careers, this is a recipe for failure. Men ought to join because of the spiritual growth they will experience, along with fellowship—not to close a deal. If brothers show up because they think they will get financial tips and build work connections, they are in the wrong place. The group's purpose is to develop one's spiritual faith in service of improving their relationships.

MONEY AND DUES

There are no dues when it comes to Power of 4. Again, we are not a mastermind or skill-building group. All volunteers, we show up because we need it and because others need it, too. We also divide the bill at the end of meals together, rotating who pays. There is no rigidness to it. It is generosity; taking your turn to serve others.

OTHER RELIGIONS WELCOME?

As renowned pastor Rick Warren has said, "It's not about religion. It's about *relationships.*" Imagine a triangle = you, your wife, and Christ. That can get you through a lot. Still, the one thing we share amongst our brothers is a mutual belief in Christ. Each of us is in Power of 4 because we need it.

When we look at whom we are with—whom we are spending time with—it's those other men who bring what we need. We participate in the group because of our commonality. It's not just that we are Christians, it's because everyone in our circle wants to be an honorable, good servant of Christ. The desires we hold are the same as pastors and lay people. We want to be in line with the will of God, empowered by the Holy Spirit.

As Steve recounts, he has been in groups where men were nominal in their beliefs. "They didn't bring value. And they didn't get much from me."

(SIGNIFICANT) AGE DIFFERENCES

Steve was once in a different men's group. A 20- and 30-year-old were involved. Back then, Steve was in his 60s. Another man, by the name of Gary, was in his 50s. Within a year both younger men had left.

Six months into meeting, the younger guys revealed that there were times when they felt lost talking to older men. They had trouble understanding them. The disparity in thinking was the culprit. The age gulf was too big. The younger men's lack of life experiences prevented them from connecting with what the older brothers were dealing with. Also, the younger brothers' priorities were different. They wanted to talk about how to get a better job, how to impress their boss, etc. This was old hat for the senior brothers. Bill and Steve were well past this period in their lives.

Still, Steve confesses he did have some affinity with the 20-year-old. Unlike the peer-to-peer connection that Power of 4 affords, Steve felt like a grandparent to this young man. In fact, he was the first person he and his wife would call when something came up with their new baby. They didn't phone their own parents. Instead, they rang Steve and his wife Linda.

Even this relationship was wanting, though. As Steve explains, "We reached down to give this young couple a helping hand, but it wasn't reciprocated. It wasn't all their fault. Their lives were too overflowing with raising their kids, running a business, and managing health issues. It's just that this young couple was more in survival mode with little margin or resources. They were young and still figuring things out."

This is a specific instance, but it represents a general issue. All four of our current Power of 4 brotherhood love each other and provide value due to our similar life stations. But if a man doesn't have the life experience to reciprocate in a relationship, they will continue to be on the learning curve rather than the application curve. Now, can a 30-year-old co-exist in a Power of 4 brotherhood with a 60-year-old? Certainly, there are younger guys willing to be mentored who then can act as a conduit to the younger generation, helping younger men catch up. When they (figuratively) sit at the feet of their elders, they can transmit precious insights to their peers.

In a related point, experience does matter. People want the experience of those around them to shorten their own problem-solving. Even the way people talk at different life stages is critical. Take the word "cool." What does "cool" mean to a 20-year-old vs. a 60-year-old? Their thoughts are bound to diverge.

Another consideration is the ages of brothers' kids. If men have children roughly the same age, it's helpful for connectivity. Kids act as a bridge. They create community structure; it's not the parents, it's the kids driving such affinity.

Knowing that each generation repeats the mistakes of the previous, one way to fix this is to bring young and old men together—within reason. As mentioned, a gulf tends to exist between men who are decades apart. There can be younger men unaffected by the age gap—who can connect with their senior brothers—but this is not always the case. Accordingly, we suggest taking it on an individual, case-by-case basis.

The Bible talks about impacting people generationally. We agree. We mustn't think about just this generation, but the next one too, and so on down the road. It also helps to avoid promoting generational trauma. As we age, we should think in bigger terms, beginning with reassessing outcomes. For instance, it's not about how you did in kindergarten. You must think about how your grandkids will fare in school.

That's what we're interested in with Power of 4.

HOW TO MIX OLD BELIEVERS WITH NEW BELIEVERS

Let's talk about new Christians vs. old Christians, beginning with our brother Keith. He dabbled in Christianity in his younger years. Later, working in the surf industry, he was considered hip, cool. But then the surf industry changed. His earnings went down. He found himself in a situation where he began questioning things.

His son was in a Christian-based organization that allowed Keith to reflect on the missing spiritual aspect to his life. He soon found he connected to Christianity more than the party lifestyle. Impassioned by a resurgence in his faith, he questioned his views on many things that he had taken for granted for a long time. In short, he was having a midlife spirituality crisis as God opened him up.

This transformation wasn't just a boon for Keith. It helped us "Old Christians" reflect on our own faith. In some ways, it's like going to Disneyland with your grandkids. You see all the same stuff you grew up loving, but with fresh eyes.

Here was Keith asking questions that many of us had

already answered. Yet, by asking them afresh or anew, it allowed us deeper contemplation. Christ is our first love; applying the previous metaphor, we had been on those rides at Disneyland before, but we hadn't done it for a while. Not only did we watch him grow, but we also *helped* him grow. This represents almost the reversal of the age challenge we just discussed. Helping a mentee in this way strengthens our bond with Christ—and with each other.

HOW TO MAKE THIS ATTRACTIVE TO YOUNGER MEN

If the prevailing culture was trying to make Power of 4 attractive to young men, they would invariably use sex. (That's our culture's go-to.) Almost every men's ministry involves the sex impulse, especially tackling so-called sex addiction these days. We're not skirting the issue in our group. Rather, we view this as a *substitute* problem. Every man's battle concerns sexual behavior and temptation. Especially so for young men.

But the core issue is character. How we handle impulses; whether they be infidelity's lure, pornography addiction, prostitution, etc. To date, we haven't focused on these other items as primary concerns for our group. Our brothers' lives are our agenda, so we haven't made these prominent points. They are secondary issues.

It's helpful to think about *The Wizard of Oz*. All of us men want different things (a heart, brain, courage, etc.), yet we are all on the same road. Even if we are talking about younger men, they need to follow the road. Three major sins continually tempt us: lust of the eyes, lust of the flesh, and the pride of life. If you are a younger person, you need to first acknowledge this struggle exists if you ever hope to not be consumed by temptation.

Of nearly equal concern is the "screens culture" that dominates the minds of so many young men. Steve has a unique approach here. Instead of making the screen an enemy of relationships, he suggests we need to reframe them as tools for connection. "I use it to keep up with my guys," he says, referring to his disciples, the young men who look up to him. "But this requires self-awareness and impulse control; learning how to use tools so they don't use you."

Power of 4 can assist with this, especially by allowing brethren to discuss best practices to combat screens' mania and the growing addiction to (online) pornography. According to *Psychology Today*, "More than 90 percent of young men report watching porn videos with some regularity, particularly in the United States. Many of these videos depict acts that they might never engage in themselves—in other words, erotic fantasies."

As we know, we need fathers that can lead by example to deal with these problems and more. Getting on the same page can prepare us to show the way for our kids concerning tech. Talking it out as a group can lead to helpful approaches. For instance, maybe you establish a structure for your family where everyone turns off their phones for a certain number of hours. Perhaps you create other boundaries or limits.

This goes back to the core issue of why Jesus chose to have three men close to Him. Our Lord purposefully gathered a group of men who encouraged and supported one another to further His ultimate mission—our salvation. Fathers of teenagers are up against their own trials when it comes to screens. No, these aren't always life-or-death situations like what Jesus faced, but that doesn't mean it's not difficult to raise a young person amongst so much (digital) temptation these days.

Having a group of committed brothers is one way to

manage the struggle. Drawing strength from one another is a critical aspect. Another one is having a sounding board for venting and formulating better approaches to the problem.

DISCIPLINED STRUCTURE VS. AN AD HOC ARRANGEMENT

We tend to like the open-ended format for organizing meetings. So long as every guy gets a turn—so long as each brother is seen and heard—you're on the right track. When Andrew first joined, he was surprised our group wasn't more like a Bible study, i.e., that we didn't open each meeting with the Bible and consult scripture when brothers raised issues in their lives. That's not our approach. Instead, it's more *relationship-oriented.* We work out our problems by listening to one another, working through challenges in the moment.

Being a small group is helpful in this regard as we require fewer rules, less structure. Mastermind groups with six to eight people, on the other hand, or large Bible study organizations, need more organization. That's not our objective. Instead, ours is to go deep. Being small in number allows you to do that. This is why we suggest keeping the number of attendees small and manageable.

Think about it this way: The size of a group creates the standard; if you have eight people, others might get antsy when they are not the focus of attention. Such a big group is also unwieldly. But you can go deeper if you have a smaller, more intimate group. In time, you will develop history together, further cementing your relationships around mutual trust.

Another consideration concerning rules is brothers' personalities. If you have all "Type-A" men, you may need more rules. And of course, if one person is not respecting the group, that may necessitate a group conversation. For instance, if one man shows up ten minutes late consistently, that may need to be addressed. Ultimately, it comes down to respect. Being punctual is a sign of caring. Not only does it indicate your commitment, but it also has practical applications, i.e., it allows meetings to run better.

What you don't want, though, is to emphasize rules over relationships. We want to be in the here and now, be fully present. If a brother is going through something hard, requiring several sessions to cover, we should grant him this. There even might be an ongoing situation requiring us to really spend some extended time (years) on something. That's okay. The real goal is to speak the truth in love to each other, not to tabulate how much time we have spent helping a brother.

In effect, we don't want the rules to be the fifth brother. We want the men to be so committed to each other, they will do whatever it takes to make things right for another man. This can require *gentle* confrontation at times to facilitate a smooth meeting flow, but it shouldn't necessitate hard and fast rules mandating the way meetings proceed.

TAKEAWAYS

Here are some more quick best practice insights:

* Consider yourself a *leaderless* group. When one brother starts calling the shots, it hinders honest 360° feedback and perspective.

* Emphasize unstructured time; the more rules you establish the stiffer and more business-like Power of 4 becomes, harming relationships.

* Proceed from a deep respect for your brothers. Allow this reverence to color everything you say or do.

* Keep conversations natural, free-flowing, and fluid. Remember: this is not a therapy session. It's a dialogue among friends and peers.

* No facilitator needed.

* No one should watch the clock. Instead, whenever someone must go is a good time to end.

* Avoid giving advice. Foster an emotional connection of understanding.

* Emphasize the share aspect. One person shares. Three others reflect it back.

* Promote the need for men to be able to be men with each other.

* No sitting on the edge, wishing to go first. Be respectful. Wait your turn.

* On the other hand, don't be so respectful that no one talks first. Someone must be the initiator.

* Think long-term. Grow together. Finish well together.

CHAPTER 12

The Questions We Wish We Had Answers to When We Started

What if someone dies in your group?

This is a replacement issue. Brothers may think it's a good idea to rush into getting another person. There's some logic to this. Having someone else in the group can lighten the load. We simply urge caution. Don't bring in someone else just to fill the void, especially if this man is likely to not be a long-term fit.

As mentioned in the last chapter, our brothers are on the older side. With recent medical advances, we'll most likely continue to meet for the foreseeable future, until each brother dies. Then again, if a brother, such as Keith, were to die in an accident before his time, Steve who is older, would most likely seek out a replacement in due time. This is reminiscent of the Biblical story of Jonathan and David. David was lost after Jonathan died and never replaced him—to his own detriment.

We want to avoid that trap.

What does personal development look like to Power of 4?

Our attitude concerns brotherhood, rather than individualized achievement. We want to be there when another man needs us, when they need to be cheered on. There is no finish line.

Each day as we age, we are improving daily in our soul. At the time of death is glorification. There is no end date to our process. Instead, it's a constant *journey* of sanctification. The more awareness we possess of our sanctification (as a gift) by the Holy Spirit, the more we can participate, using this influence for the betterment of others.

It's not about us achieving or getting to a new level. It's about us helping others on their own path. Development is about the deepening of our relationship with the Holy Spirit and determining how to let it guide us in each moment, especially so we don't miss opportunities to care for others.

Do you judge brothers for their actions?

How can you be in a true brotherhood when you aren't coming ugly? (If you are lying to yourself or others.) Here's an example: A lacrosse player Mark knows won't take responsibility for his life. He's 27 years old and still acts like the high schooler Mark once coached. Recently, he called Mark. "I really want you to mentor me now," he said. But Mark is in communication with this young man's other buddies and knows he's drinking and acting out in irresponsible ways. Mark said, "I cannot mentor you until you get sober."

The young man was unwilling to do the work or be honest, so Mark couldn't help him. This situation is no outlier. A lot of men (some much older than this former lacrosse player) refuse to be grownups, to take responsibility for their lives. They need to step up to the plate.

There's another important consideration. Our group is not mentor-mentee. *We're on the same level.* If our fellow brothers aren't truthful with each other, if we're just playing games, we're setting ourselves up for a kill shot from Satan.

Satan will take us out and many others by fear. Ephesians 6:10-24 states: If you don't put on God's armor you cannot stand up against the principalities of this world. Remember, Jesus chose three men to be in His inner circle for His mission's legacy. Also, if we profess to mentor others but don't hold ourselves accountable, we set up the whole platoon for destruction.

Why not two brothers? Or five?

In Mark 2:1-12, there's a story about a paralytic who couldn't get into a house to see Jesus of his own accord:

> When Jesus came back to Capernaum a few days later, it was heard that He was at home. And many were gathered together, so that there was no longer space, not even near the door; and He was speaking the word to them. And some people came, bringing to Him a man who was paralyzed, carried by four men. And when they were unable to get to Him because of the crowd, they removed the roof above Him; and after digging an opening, they let down the pallet on which the paralyzed man was lying. And Jesus, seeing their faith, said to the paralyzed man, "Son, your sins are forgiven. (Mark 2:1-5, NASB)"

Our Lord healed the paralytic man due to the faith of the four men who brought him in. As we have stated often, there's power in the number four. In the last chapter we explained how Jesus chose three men close beside Him for His ordeal. If it was good enough for the Lord, it's good for us.

We strive to be a strong group of four, but the group *can* work with more brothers. For now, we would like to break down how having more men in your corner can help you as a man.

ONE MAN
He must stand on his own. Bereft of allies, he must deal with his challenges all by himself.

TWO MEN
Our man now has a friend who cares for him. If he falls, his buddy can pick him up, and vice versa. Iron sharpens iron. Each can act on the other, challenging him to do better.

THREE MEN
We now have a triangle situation. Ideal for teamwork, when a task is handed to the trio they can come at it from different angles, offering a 360° perspective. They can also increase their personal skills and talents because they are a team, increasing chances for success.

FOUR MEN
Three make a triangle, but with four, you have one person in the center. The three possess a 360° view of someone's life, offering invaluable insights. Together, the four can become who they were created to be.

FIVE MEN
All the benefits of having four men are present; it just takes maturity and experience to manage this number of men right.

The time each person must share with the group will be divided by five, so there are fewer opportunities to focus on each brother. Still, the more strands on the rope, the stronger it gets. (Note: We have had five brothers in our group at times; if we began with five brothers, it would have been much harder to manage at the outset due to the additional complexity.)

What about men who are busy dealing with things like kids and work?

They can *still* do this. In fact, it's even more critical for these men. The seeds you are sowing now will bear fruit later. If you don't invest in this stuff now, where will you be in a few decades when you really need it? You may think you are too busy to meet with men for one to two hours a week in this difficult and often overbooked time, but it's akin to meditation. People who say "I don't have 20 minutes a day" should really be doing it 40 minutes daily.

You also need to get involved earlier rather than later because it's an investment. Not only in yourself but in the health and well-being of your family. Your brothers will keep you accountable. They'll hold up a mirror to you. And they'll keep you on a godly path, especially when you have the tendency to stray as things get harder in these crunch years.

Still on the fence? Picture Steve in 1972, the first year he was in Power of 4. Back then he had two kids, ages three and five. He was the youngest brother of his group. They met for one hour on Tuesday mornings at 6:30 AM.

This used to be Steve's least favorite time of day. It became his golden hour. "It was because of that time that I was stabilized for the rest of my week," he says. "It was such a good experience that when we did break up after two and a half years, I knew why I had to continue to meet with other men. Alone, I didn't have a spiritual navigation system. And I couldn't see myself facing the choices I had to make without these brothers around me. I needed their advice and knew I could give it back."

Bottom line: invest the time and energy now. You may not think you have the bandwidth, but you are wrong. Establishing these connections will keep you on the right path for the (challenging) years to come.

What about the guy who's scared to share?

You must walk through the pain of becoming vulnerable. The idea, that if you were to tell people who you really are then they would hurt you because you had allowed vulnerability, is a lie. Spoiler alert: others are scared to be hurt too. Do this together; it makes it easier.

How do you vet prospects?

Our answer is: "It depends." In Keith's case, he was in crisis. We decided to bring him on even though another brother expressed concerns about him joining. We put in a protocol to make sure everything was confidential to alleviate concerns. To keep things simple, Steve has a short questionnaire. Actually, it consists of two questions:

1. What do you bring to the table that will benefit the other guys?

2. What do you need the guys to bring to you?

What are warning signs a man won't be a good fit?

One of the prospects Steve met with some years back wore a winter coat during their entire session. He never took it off. "He was so scared of being vulnerable that this was the outward behavior demonstrating his reluctance," explains Steve. We advise looking for similar warning signs and trusting your gut. When it comes to voting a candidate in, the decision needn't be unanimous but if someone has legitimate concerns, we advise hearing them out.

What is your stance on guests?

There have been times when our kids or grandkids have popped in for a meeting. And every now and then someone from out of town may come visit. We are open for the occasional drop-in. But we tend to not go too deep in these meetings for obvious reasons. Steve would like to introduce all his grandsons to the group but hasn't pushed it because he knows that the fun that they might have would undermine the main purpose. Instead, he wants to be sensitive to the other brothers, as he knows our time together is important to their spiritual growth and doesn't want that diminished.

Are you cool with women joining?

Steve has been asked this question many times over the years. It's a natural consideration on the part of females, especially when they observe positive transformations amongst the men who belong to Power of 4.

Whenever they ask to join us, Steve has a ready answer: "Go start your own group."

To date, none have.

Margy, Mark's wife, enjoys a nice relationship with Steve. The other day she, Mark, and Steve all went to lunch. Mark watched her dote over Steve. This isn't the first time either. They are so close, in part because of the positive changes she has seen in Mark through the group. While they enjoyed this time together, Margy also understands boundaries. She's not interested in pulling away her husband and his friends from an activity that brings such meaning, purpose, and joy to their lives.

Back in the early days, Power of 4 hosted family beach days

featuring football in the sand. It was at one of these that the other guys met Linda, Steve's wife, for the first time. And Power of 4 also hosted Mark's 25th anniversary to great success. The two renewed their vows amongst the families of brothers. It helps to be inclusive but it's also important to remember boundaries.

CHAPTER 13

What Our Families Say About Power of 4

Throughout this book, you've read a lot about why Power of 4 came together and what keeps us going. You've read stories about brothers describing how our group helped them face problems, big and small. You've learned how transparency and authenticity enabled our fellow men to grow as responsible individuals, committed to positively impacting the next generation(s). We've also discussed how it's possible to break past cycles of addiction or chains of poor behavior by creating *new* healthy behaviors—through walking closer with God.

Each brother turns to Power of 4 to gain external perspectives on their internal situation, so it's fitting to close our discussion with outside perspectives on our group itself. While writing these pages, we collected feedback from our wives and children, along with the families of selected former brothers. We accomplished this using a third party to anonymously gather opinions.

Why do it anonymously? That's simple. We expected our families to feel positively about our group, but it's still human nature to pull punches when it's someone we love requesting input. By keeping comments anonymous, we've allowed for honesty, not to mention, tried to remove any friction over which statements were included and which were left on the cutting room floor!

Ultimately, we rely on Power of 4 to help us become better men. Part of being a good man is being a good husband and father, so without further ado, let's consider what our loved ones have to say.

ON LISTENING TO OUR WIVES

Socrates once said, "By all means marry; if you get a good wife, you'll become happy; if you get a bad one, you'll become a philosopher." We're pleased to say there isn't a single philosopher amongst Power of 4, which means we all chose wisely in the wife department.

Our first spouse's comments remind us of the Bible's stance on companionship:

> Two are better than one because they have a good return for their labor; for if either of them falls, the one will lift up his companion. But woe to the one who falls when there is not another to lift him up! (Ecclesiastes 4:9-10, NASB)

The above can, in one sense, apply to marriage, but it can also certainly pertain to the greater brotherhood of men in Power of 4. Here's what she said:

> To say Power of 4 has had an incredible impact on my husband would be a gross understatement. He has been in this group of godly, serving men for more than a decade. I can honestly say that I credit these men for keeping our marriage healthy and strong,

and if I'm perfectly honest, they have helped to keep our marriage together.

The men have done this by constantly sharing God's truth and wisdom for marriage with my husband, as well as their life experiences. This, coupled with love, guidance, accountability, and mercy, has helped my husband and I stay on track during many difficult and desperate times. Not only has this group helped our marriage thrive, but they have also helped with the day-to-day complexities of raising children, and well, just living life in general.

Here's another related comment from a spouse:

With the guiding principles of Power of 4 being based on the Bible and shared monthly with my husband, his general mental, emotional, and spiritual health has improved beyond measure. He has grown and matured significantly in every aspect of life, and I and our children have been the recipient of this beautiful growth. Beyond a shadow of doubt, we are more committed to each other and to our family. We quickly take care of any issues that may arise, and we celebrate the good daily.

And another:

We are more grateful for one another and, to put it simply, we have a better foundation. This is all because of the wise counsel that he receives during his Power of 4 fellowship. Our marriage is solidly based on God's truth, a principle of the group, and we are healthier and happier because of it.

One Power of 4 wife finds great value in the group being a "safe harbor" where her husband can discuss anything on his mind without fear of judgement, upsetting his family, or losing community status. She reflects on how our group plays a vital role in fulfilling a biblical instruction:

> Bear one another's burdens, and thereby fulfill the law of Christ. (Galatians 6:2, NASB)

She writes:

> My sense of Power of 4 is that it is a group of godly, Christ-centered men, who are completely committed to each other and meet on a regular basis for the betterment of all. During their time together they have the freedom to speak openly and honestly about everything that is happening in their life; the good, the bad, and sometimes, the ugly.
>
> My husband needs that kind of safe harbor to discuss anything that is on his mind. These men, with biblical guidance, work through life together. It's pretty beautiful! With the love of this group, my husband has been able to receive healing and clarity in many of the things that have been challenging him, and because of this I and our children, as well as his various communities, are recipients of his healthy growth and fresh perspective.

Here's another related perspective from a wife who has seen positive changes in her spouse:

> Some challenges are new, but many of them are old, and our entire family has experienced a deliverance

from past bondage with his participation with the group. With Power of 4, he has built up and worked on his integrity, honesty, love, mercy, compassion, patience, living in the truth, accountability, and knowledge of who God is in his life.

A spouse of a former brother commented on the usefulness of Power of 4 for men everywhere. Indeed, her husband set up a group modeled on Power of 4 after their move out of state. She included in her response two Bible verses that inform her view:

Where there is no guidance the people fall, but in an abundance of counselors there is victory. (Proverbs 11:14, NASB)

Be devoted to one another in brotherly love; give preference to one another in honor. (Romans 12:10, NASB)

On the importance of Power of 4 groups for men, she writes:

I think such brotherhood can and will be extremely helpful to other men especially in the world in which we are living today. The truth is, life can be difficult. Our world is changing so quickly that it's hard to keep a firm footing no matter how you have prepared yourself, how strong you are, and no matter how knowledgeable and capable you are.

Here's another similar remark we received:

Power of 4 brings a clear and concise biblical mindset
and good fundamental practice to men to aid them
in their daily walk. To have a refuge where they "fit"
and where they are able to discuss openly and hon-
estly all the things they face in their life is crucial.
Men need this! To be encouraged by other men who
may be experiencing the same joys and struggles you
are experiencing is life-giving and affirming. To know
that you are not alone with your questions, thoughts,
desires, struggles, and disappointments is vital. The
benefits of this small, intimate, group of men from
all backgrounds and of all ages is far-reaching and is
the type of community that must be available for all
Christian men.

One wife focused her answer on the spirituality and faith
guiding of Power of 4. She pointed to a different verse to
frame her answer:

That is, that I may be encouraged together with you
while among you, each of us by the other's faith, both
yours and mine. (Romans 1:12, NASB)

She explains:

Power of 4 is all about faith and spirituality. If you
are walking with this group of men, your focus is on
God's holy scripture and what His desire is for your
life. The affirmation and encouragement, as well as a
healthy dose of accountability, that you receive from
this group only deepens your knowledge and love of
Christ. It is a biblically-based love, making wisdom

and spiritual growth a natural byproduct of this fellowship.

One spouse believes Power of 4 is more important today than it was when it was founded almost 20 years ago. She also looks to the Bible for inspiration:

Therefore, encourage one another and build one another up, just as you also are doing. (1 Thessalonians 5:11, NASB)

She writes:

Power of 4 is desperately needed now more than ever in this moment in time. You cannot watch or read any news story and not realize how out of focus and lost our nation and world is and that we are headed for destruction. We have become a confused, hateful, godless society; one with no morals, consideration or respect for anything or anyone. This is a tragic time in our history.

Part of the reason for this is that the roles of our husbands, fathers, sons, and friends have been so grossly eroded that there is very little left of the male gender as we know it. Our men have been kicked to the curb and silenced, and all their capacity to lead, serve, and care for their communities has been diminished and degraded simply because they are men. This is tragic. We need our men back. Our families and communities are starving for truthful, godly, male leadership. Power of 4 will help bring back biblical order and principles that our society as a whole desperately needs.

Along similar lines, another spouse put it this way:

> Power of 4 gives security, honor, respect, encourage-
> ment, godly principles, understanding, and hope for
> the complex situations that occur in life. Men need
> to have other men to laugh and to cry with, to share
> their greatest joys, sorrows, difficulties, desires, ex-
> pectations, and dreams with. Men need strong, godly,
> male friendships that they can navigate life with, and
> Power of 4 is just that group.

She added a final comment underscoring her view of the group:

> Power of 4 is a fortress.

The wife of one brother feels the group has been tremendously helpful in his life. She writes:

> It feels like it has been a very positive experience for
> my husband, finding a support system with the men
> in his group. I believe they have been a huge support
> to him, and that's invaluable. The group has helped
> him in building confidence and making a connec-
> tion with other men that are going through similar
> (or not so similar) stuff.

She explains her overall view on the group by saying:

> My sense of Power of 4 is that it creates a safe circle
> to share and to be supported, while also having the
> knowledge and experiences of the men in the group;

sharing resources, networking, meeting new people, and making contacts. It's another resource for navigating the journey. It's had a tremendously positive impact on our family that is renewed with every meeting.

When asked why Power of 4 has been so valuable to her husband, one wife explains:

There is a lot going on in the world. And it all seems overwhelming. It is always good to have a group of friends you can talk to about everything, personal and worldly. A man sharing his faith with a group of men he respects, hearing their perspectives and sharing his in turn, seems like a wonderful way to strengthen your faith.

LISTENING TO OUR CHILDREN

As you might expect, the kids who provided their input did so with much shorter answers—they're used to replying via emojis and text messages. Despite writing pithier responses, the children of brothers who responded provided an insightful view of how Power of 4 impacts the lives of family members who live with our brothers.

One daughter explained the importance of Power of 4 for her father:

I really appreciate knowing that my dad has a group with whom he can safely and openly share about all aspects of his life. It's hard for men to find that and I have been thankful to know he has had their support during some difficult times.

A son answered in a similar manner, placing emphasis on the ability of men to reveal their true thoughts and feelings. He said:

> I can't think of any other time in my dad's life where he's had the ability to share things consistently and openly with a trusted group. I know that has brought a great deal of peace, solidarity, and encouragement to him, which has reflected in all parts of his life.

One adult child observed firsthand the way brothers act in anticipation of a Power of 4 meeting, explaining:

> I had breakfast with Power of 4 once and I could sense the relief from each man because of the opportunity to be around each other again. I think there's a sense of relief and a looking forward to meetings when things are good/bad in life, because they know they have a place where they can process it all. I imagine all the families have sensed the positive impact of the group.

A college-aged son explained his view on how Power of 4 can be helpful to other Christian men, writing:

> I think Power of 4 dismantles the idea that men need to be strong and suppress feelings. It's a healthy way for men to express feelings, emotions, and struggles in a safe way. This makes men less isolated. Men feel limited with whom they can share information, but the group is a safe way to share all parts of their lives, including matters of faith.

Echoing statements of others, one child of a former brother believes Power of 4 is more important in today's world than ever before. She writes:

> I think that this group is a vital piece of the puzzle in a world that is ever changing. A group like Power of 4 ensures that nothing is out of whack and helps the man holistically in a world that is facing many challenges and can feel overwhelming. It's a super healthy way for men to be in touch with their emotions and express them in a positive way. It's a safe place where men don't have to worry about vulnerability but instead can embrace it.

WHAT ARE YOU WAITING FOR?

The comments from our families are tremendously gratifying. They see the same benefits of Power of 4 that we do. We come to every meeting striving to be better husbands and fathers, and our families see this dedication reflected in how we act with them. Every one of us thank God for our wonderful families and the chance to be better for them daily.

By now, you've read our stories and what our families have to say. There are just two questions remaining on the last page of this book:

1. What are you waiting for?

2. When will you form your own Power of 4 and experience the many benefits we (and our families) just described?

Please think on it. Pray on it. And get your invitations out there!

START YOUR OWN
POWER OF 4 NOW

Here's the link: www.powerof4.co

On the website, you can interact with us and find the tools to increase the impact of your Power of 4 experience.

* Sign up to receive the FREE Power of 4 updates.

* Purchase Power of 4 books to give to other men.

* Select the Power of 4 Workbook Starter Kit that will guide your new brotherhood through your first 12 sessions.

* Order the one-on-one Mentoring Red Letter Discussions from the Book of Matthew.

Mentoring is the second step of the Power of 4 program, influencing young men to discover, discuss, and decide the place Jesus' teachings and life have in our modern world.

**Your Power of 4 will support you to
"Finish well, together!"**

ABOUT THE AUTHORS

Mark Warren

A devoted family man, Mark Warren has been married to his best friend Margy for over 35 years. They have two adult children that are now (happily) off the payroll. Mark has long loved water sports, especially surfing and has traveled to many off-the-grid spots to enjoy the creations God has set before us.

A sought-after corporate industry speaker and trainer, he serves as a Managing Director at one of the oldest investment companies in America. Mark joined his firm in 1990 and possesses more than 30 years of investor experience in the financial services industry.

Prior to his professional success, Mark earned both a Master of Business Administration degree in marketing and a bachelor's degree from the University of San Diego. For the last three decades he has enabled his clients to retire with dignity, educate their children, and bequeath legacies, if so desired. Mark has also mentored young men at the high school level as a lacrosse coach and prepared young minds for college and internships after graduation.

Dr. Steven D. Bagley

Steve writes, records, and videos about grief and men. He has produced many articles, as well as his book *Never Alone*, telling the story about the loss of his wife after 43 years of marriage. *Power of 4* comes out of Steve's 50 years of experience, beginning in 1972 when he joined three other men who shared struggles, applying Jesus' teachings to their lives, and supporting one another. Steve has two adult children: A son and daughter, along with seven grandchildren.

Steve's holds a bachelor's degree with a double major in Psychology and Christian Education from Azusa Pacific University. He received his master's degree in Christian Education from Talbot Seminary and received his Ph.D. in Marriage and Family Therapy from California Graduate Institute.

After serving the church as a pastoral staff member for 20 years, Steve became the COO of Alpha Counseling Center. He guided 60 out-patient therapists, serving six Southern California counties, and helped design four in-patient Christian treatment programs. Steve then founded Marriage & Family Matters Counseling in 1991 with his beloved late wife Linda, the Clinical Director and Supervisor. They led this Christian counseling and training center until Linda's unexpected dead in 2013.

In 2002, Steve joined Arms of Love International's Board of Directors, operating children's homes for orphaned and at-risk children in Nicaragua and the Philippines. From 2014–2018, Steve was the President and Board Chairman. He has also served the Kojo Church network in Tokyo, Japan for 15 years, training ministers in counseling, small group development, and men's ministry. (He leveraged business community ministry opportunities for evangelism in a gospel-resistant culture.)

Michael Ashley

A columnist with *Forbes, Entrepreneur,* and *Becker's Health Review,* Michael has written nearly 50 books on many subjects, including 4 bestsellers. His many books have been published by Wiley & Sons, Simon & Schuster, Quarto, Fast Company Press, and McGraw Hill. A former Disney screenwriter and college professor of writing, his work has appeared in *Fox Sports, Huffpost, Entertainment Weekly, The National Examiner,* the United Nations' *ITU News, The Orange County Register,* and *The Orange County Business Journal.*

Michael is a professional speaker who keynotes and conduct workshops for national organizations, including ProVisors and Vistage. The father of two exceptional young boys, Michael is married to the love of his life and lives in North Idaho.

Made in the USA
Monee, IL
21 March 2024